March 17th

A hopeful Guide to
your Life's journey!

Love Always
&
Forever
Dad

GUIDE
MY
FEET

GUIDE MY FEET

Guide my feet while I run this race.

Guide my feet while I run this race.

Guide my feet while I run this race, for I

don't want to run this race in vain.

Guide my feet while I run this race,
   for I don't want to run this race in vain.

I'm Your child while I run this race,
   for I don't want to run this race in vain.

Search my heart while I run this race,
   for I don't want to run this race in vain.

Stand by me while I run this race,
   for I don't want to run this race in vain.

Hold my hand while I run this race,
   for I don't want to run this race in vain.

Guide my feet while I run this race,
   for I don't want to run this race in vain.

— *Negro spiritual*

GUIDE MY FEET

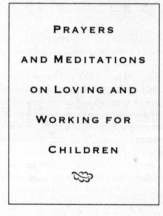

PRAYERS

AND MEDITATIONS

ON LOVING AND

WORKING FOR

CHILDREN

MARIAN WRIGHT EDELMAN

HarperPerennial

A Division of HarperCollins*Publishers*

This book was originally published in 1995 by Beacon Press. It is here reprinted by permission of Beacon Press.

GUIDE MY FEET. Copyright © 1995 by Marian Wright Edelman. All rights reserved. Printed in the United States of America. No part of this book may be used or reproduced in any manner whatsoever without written permission except in the case of brief quotations embodied in critical articles and reviews. For information, address Beacon Press, Inc., 25 Beacon Street, Boston, MA 02108-2892.

HarperCollins books may be purchased for educational, business, or sales promotional use. For information please write: Special Markets Department, HarperCollins Publishers, Inc., 10 East 53rd Street, New York, NY 10022.

First HarperPerennial edition published 1996.

Designed by Anne Chalmers
Composition by Wilstead & Taylor

ISBN 0-06-097711-6 (pbk.)

96 97 98 99 00 HC 10 9 8 7 6 5 4 3 2 1

ACKNOWLEDGMENTS

I am deeply grateful for the patient and constructive reading and help of Shannon Daley and Enola Aird and of my editor at Beacon, Deanne Urmy. I am also grateful for the wonderful Children's Sabbath litanies prepared by Shannon and the Safe Start covenant written by Enola. I am equally grateful for the ever-cheerful assistance and hard work of Donna Jablonski, Ellen Brown Ngalieu, and Ivanna Weikert Omeechevarria.

Thanks too to Beth and Charles Miller, Deborah Szekely, Peter and Eileen Norton, and Arthur and Marylin Levitt, for beautiful and quiet spaces to write.

As always, I am grateful to and for my family, especially my husband Peter, whose patience and love enable me to juggle home, work, and community responsibilities.

And I am grateful to God for everything.

This book is dedicated to
my three children—Joshua, Jonah, and Ezra,
who are the lights of my life—
and to all children.

It is also dedicated to all those
committed workers and leaders for
children, whose hands, minds, feet, voices,
and efforts will assure that one day
no child will be left behind.

CONTENTS

GUIDE MY FEET

◎ I SET OUT to write a very different book — a policy book — but out tumbled prayers instead.

A long time ago when I read that Martin Luther prayed four hours a day, I wondered how he found the time. It was, he said, the only way he could gain enough strength to carry on his work. As I have grown older and wearier trying to help get our nation to put children first and become more worried about my own and other people's children growing up in an America where moral and common sense and family and community values are disintegrating, I pray more and more. I know that only with God's help and only with prayer, which Gandhi called "the key of the morning and the bolt of the evening," can some mountains be moved. In this book, I share my struggles through prayer as a parent, as a person of faith, and as a child advocate.

As I contemplate the kind of future I want for children — my own and other people's — I believe we must look inward to God for guidance and strength and backward to draw on the values and legacies of our families, ancestors, and communities. After many challenges and successes in over three decades of service to children, again and again I have drawn on my childhood experiences when family, church, the extended community family, and teachers provided a seamless web of support for Black children. Although stigmatized and devalued by the external world in an era of racial apartheid, when government not only did not help but hindered, Black adults refused to let external barriers become internal ones. They wrapped children in a cocoon of caring and activity. And they knew that the care of the mind and the body needed to be grounded in the care of the spirit, which was the glue that held our families and our community together.

Every Sunday morning my parents, sister, three brothers, and I gathered around the breakfast table. Each child had to recite a Bible verse before our family repeated the Lord's Prayer together. We could get away with "Jesus wept" only once! After breakfast, we brushed our teeth, combed our hair, dressed up in our best clothes, checked out our appearances in the mirror and with each other, and went off to Sunday school and to Shiloh Baptist Church. Daddy was the pastor and Mama was the church organist and choir director. After church we drove elderly or disabled parishioners home and then prepared and ate dinner together. While my mother fried or "smothered" chicken or pork chops, we children took turns churning ice cream for dessert, setting the table, and entertaining any guests invited to join us for Sunday dinner in our church parsonage. On communion Sunday, once a month, I eagerly rushed before dinner to the church kitchen to help clean up the communion trays so I could drink all the tiny glasses of grape juice, a luxury in my home that I could never get enough of. I'd leave just enough untouched glasses for Daddy to take to give communion to the sick and shut-in.

Every Sunday afternoon, we took flowers from the church to the hospital and visited members of the congregation who were sick at home. Sunday evenings always were shared with one church member's family or another, who prepared scrumptious suppers for our family. My favorite Sunday evening was at Miz Tee Kelly's, whose fried chicken and biscuits and sweet potato pone nobody else has *ever* matched. Black church folk during my childhood in Bennettsville, South Carolina, loved their pastors, treated them like royalty, and competed to see who could out-cook and out-do the others in providing hospitality for a pastor's family.

Every schoolday morning we got up to the smells of breakfast cooking and came home every afternoon to a hot dinner and discussions about our day. After cleaning up the kitchen, we did our homework and went out in the yard to play marbles, dodgeball, horseshoes, red light, Mama May I, regular jump rope or double-dutch, hide-and-seek, and hopscotch. We had a snack, read or played a game of jacks, Old Maid, Monopoly, Chinese checkers, or pickup sticks, had our sponge baths, said our prayers, and went to bed about nine o'clock to get ready for another day.

We had fun without a lot of money, making up games that didn't need store-bought toys, money, or directions from adults. Regular checkers played with soft drink bottle caps, homemade stilts from discarded pieces of wood, or tin cans attached to wire were as much or more fun as any expensive toys we parents feel the need to buy our children today. Pin the Tail on the Donkey tickled our young funnybones for hours, and as we got older Spin the Bottle titillated our adolescent libidos, which were kept in check by everpresent adults.

Books were always a part of our home life. My parents considered them necessities rather than luxuries. Indeed, a new book was more important than a second pair of shoes. I loved to visit my daddy's book-lined study where he read for many hours of the day. And our house had piles of magazines like *Time* and *Life* and the *Saturday Evening Post* and the *Christian Century* as well as the latest in church music. Along with the daily White newspapers, Black newspapers — the *Afro-American* and the Pittsburgh *Courier* — and

Black magazines like *Ebony* and *Sepia* kept us abreast of Black community news.

On weekends, all the children had to help clean the house, the car, the yard, do errands like grocery shopping with our parents, help our daddy prepare the bulletin for Sunday service, and work with the sexton to clean up the church and churchyard. My daddy could not stand to see trash littering anything. A child's protest that we did not put it there was met with: "Pick it up anyway—it doesn't matter who put it there, it spoils our yard!"

Every day in our segregated and very unequally funded Black school, we pledged allegiance to the flag of the United States of America—"to one nation under God, indivisible, with liberty and justice for all"—and sang *every* verse of "Lift Every Voice and Sing," the Negro national anthem by James Weldon Johnson, which reminded us of "the faith that the dark past has taught us and the hope that the present has brought us."

In junior high, we memorized and recited the Gettysburg Address before our class, and in the eleventh grade every student participated in an oratorical contest. Winners displayed their rhetorical stuff before parents and the whole community. This helped children gain confidence to speak in public, and enabled us to learn about and be inspired by Black history and the rich legacy of Black struggle and achievement.

I picked a speech Ralph Bunche gave at Fisk University in the 1940s entitled "The Barriers of Race Can Be Surmounted," and I think about that speech still on days when I doubt it. Today the millions of poor Black children growing up in single-parent households could draw strength and inspiration from the remarkable achievements of Bunche, our first Black Nobel Peace Prize Laureate, who spent a significant part of his childhood years in a poor, mother-only household, and, after her death, with his grandmother, who expected and helped him to achieve and to be proud of his racial heritage. Neither being orphaned nor spending his adolescence in segregated Los Angeles, where racial stereotyping and discrimination required him to get into UCLA by his outstanding athletic skills rather than by his intellectual prowess, stopped him from turning his family losses and racial barriers into badges of distinction as he fought tirelessly for civil rights and traveled the globe in pursuit of peace on behalf of the United Nations, especially in the Middle East.

Too many Black adults today have not taught our children about their great heritage — about the kings and queens of courage and achievement who overcame slavery and segregation and helped make our land fairer for all Americans. Too many children never have heard of Medgar Evers, who died so that they could vote and sit where they want in public spaces. Too many have never read or spoken the eloquent words of Black Nobel Peace Laureates like Bunche, Martin Luther King, Jr., Chief Albert Luthuli, Desmond Tutu, and Nelson Mandela, or basked in the literary genius of Nobel Laureates Wole Soyinka, Derek Walcott, and Toni Morrison. They've not fought and overcome slavery with Harriet Tubman, Sojourner Truth, and Frederick Douglass, or wrestled segregation to the ground with Fannie Lou Hamer, Thurgood Marshall, and Rosa Parks. They don't know how Black children and youths withstood bombings and fire hoses in Birmingham, mobs in Little Rock, Nashville, and Jackson, and taunts and jeers in Greensboro to overcome segregation and discrimination with moral courage rather than with guns. They have not read Benjamin Mays's and Mary McLeod Bethune's words telling them they can do anything and overcome any odds. They have not prayed with Paul Laurence Dunbar, James Weldon Johnson, or Howard Thurman, or laughed and cried with Langston Hughes's "Simple."

At Brownie and Girl Scout meetings throughout the year—my troop leader was my seventh-grade teacher—I pledged to do my very best for God, my country, and fellow human beings. Scout meetings were held in her home or at church, which was the year-round hub of child, family, and community life.

Vacation Bible School week was one of our two summer highlights as we robustly sang rounds about John Brown's body and Michael rowing his boat ashore, and asked God to "Kum ba ya, Kum ba ya." The other highlight was the week of revival meetings when great Black preachers visited and lifted us beyond our daily small-town routines, work grinds, and struggles. We children watched in wonder, and often with uncontrollable giggles, as the Holy Spirit lifted some of the old church folks from their pews as they erupted in joyful shouts and dances to God with intricate rhythmic steps the envy of Bojangles and Gregory Hines.

The "Amen Corner" singers, led by Miz Sylvia Rivers's piercingly clear, steely voice, blended the chords of our slave forebears' spirituals into an *a capella* church-wide harmonic choir of heavenly fugues the great Black composers like Nathaniel Dett, Fisk's John W. Work, Morehouse's Kemper Harreld, Tuskegee's William Dawson, and Spelman's Willis Laurence James could scarcely capture on paper. "Let everybody say Aaa-men, Aaa-men, A-a-men, A-men, A-men."

After the hour or so of singing warmed our spirits and after the visiting preachers' sermons scared us to death about the wages of sin, unsaved young people (and a few desperate older sinners) went to the mourners' bench, dropped to their knees panting and praying, and fervently begged God for salvation, while congregation members clapped and sang over them, urging Jesus to come and save their souls. Although my daddy disapproved of the mourners' bench, with its "whooping and hollering," I tried it one night. I felt smothered, bothered by the noise and pressured by the heat and insistent urgings of the clapping hordes to find God. God chose instead to lift me very quietly and unexpectedly from my pew one Sunday morning when I was twelve, to walk me to the front of the church to stand beside my waiting daddy, and give Him my life.

We Black children were wrapped up and rocked in a cradle of faith, song, prayer, ritual, and worship which immunized our spirits against some of the meanness and unfairness inflicted on our young psyches by racial discrimination and poverty in our segregated South and acquiescent nation. When Detroit's great preacher Dynamo Campbell, one of my favorites, came for revival, he took us down into the Valley of Dry Bones with Ezekiel, where God asked, "Mortal, can these bones live?" and Ezekiel and Dynamo answered, "O Lord God, You know." With excitement, we collectively experienced God breathing life into and connecting those dry bones limb by limb as Dynamo strutted up and down the aisle connecting the neck bone to the shoulder bone and the hip bone to the thigh bone and the leg bone to the ankle bone and the ankle bone to the foot bone and we all emerged invigorated new people. We internalized the presence of a God, personal as well as universal, who could open our earthly graves, snatch us from death's cold hands, lift us out of misery and despair, and breathe a new spirit of life into us.

On other nights after Dynamo and Daniel's God delivered us from the lion's den, rescued Shadrach, Meshach, and Abednego from the fiery furnace, saved

Joseph from the evil jealousy of his brothers and the treachery of Potiphar's wife, parted the Red Sea for Moses and the Hebrew children, helped Joshua fight the battle of Jericho, and guided Harriet Tubman and Black slaves to freedom, we knew once and for all that *our* God—the God of our parents and grandparents and their parents and our preachers and church elders—was mighty indeed and able to deflect any threat or overcome any injustice however hard or impossible the odds appeared to our puny human eyes.

At 6:30 every morning at Spelman College, bells awakened us for breakfast and another day of study. At 7:45 A.M. chimes beckoned us to daily worship. "Faith of Our Fathers" (and Mothers), "Lord Make Me More Holy," "In Christ There Is No East or West," and other familiar hymns of childhood rang in our ears as we walked across campus to beautiful Sisters Chapel, which grounded college life.

During Sunday vespers, Willis Laurence James led the Spelman chorus and Sisters Chapel audience in an *a capella* rendering of a spiritual connecting us to our ancestral past while asking God to "guide my feet while I run this race" today. When my spirit is too depressed and arid to pray with words, King David's 90th Psalm "Lord Thou Hast Been Our Dwelling Place in All Generations," which Dr. James put to music for the Spelman chorus, soothes my soul. When I am frantic about how I am going to get through my week, I sing the Apostle Matthew's "Consider the Lilies of the Field," as I once did in Spelman's chapel, and am reminded that "sufficient unto the day is the evil thereof." It helps me do what is at hand rather than worry about what has to be done tomorrow and next week, and prompts me to remember that God knows and will meet our needs if we will but trust Him.

I was lucky not only to sing in Spelman's wonderful chorus but to be one of eight Spelman students who joined eight Morehouse students in the Sunday morning chapel choir, directed by the late and gifted Wendell Whalum. Morehouse's chapel, like Spelman's, was rich not only in music but in eloquence and in wisdom. Its president, Dr. Benjamin Mays, Martin Luther King, Jr.'s mentor, and other inspirational speakers shared with us what they believed, had experienced, and thought we needed to know to make it in the world and to make the world a better place by not becoming like the world. No idea was too big and no detail was too small to share with us as these great people and speakers prepared us to wade into the river of life with sturdy boats and oars and life vests to keep us afloat if we fell into rough waters.

They taught us to be neither victims nor victimizers; they urged us not to hate White folks because God created White folks and Black folks and Brown folks and all folks out of the same dust and would hold us — and them — ultimately to the same standards of justice. They preached that service to community was a higher value than service to self, that conscience took precedence over career, that respect for life — our own and others — was inviolate. And they taught us to value and respect ourselves and others by valuing and respecting us enough to carefully plan and prepare the daily rituals of fellowship, homework, community activities, and support at each stage of our development. When we got scared, we had someone to talk to. When we tested our wings by sitting in and picketing to challenge segregation, adults supported and shared our protests — including Dr. King — and countered the inevitable grumblers and opposition of those who object to any change and any new leadership and who seek to hang onto their comfortable status quo.

Morehouse men, like Spelman women, were taught how to dress neatly and inexpensively, to sit up straight, say yes ma'am and no ma'am, thank you and please, look people in the eye, shake hands firmly, speak clearly, and stand up when an elder entered the room. Morehouse men were even counseled — with humorous seriousness — how to woo the hearts of Spelman women by holding the door open for them to enter first and getting up and giving them their seats! What a contrast these teachings present to the filthy, disrespectful, and misogynistic lyrics of Snoop Doggy Dogg and Dr. Dre and others who shamelessly dishonor our foremothers, grandmothers, mothers, sisters, and daughters by referring to them as "hos" and "bitches." The shame of those who buy this debasing music is matched or exceeded only by those who profit so greatly from it—the record companies and the performers. How far we have plunged from Ralph Bunche and Benjamin Mays and Mary McLeod Bethune as role models to the Hollywoodized and TV-ized synthetic heroes- and heroines-for-a-day in our profit- and celebrity-crazed manufactured culture. It is time for parents and preachers and teachers and community leaders to fill the huge moral and guidance vacuum that gangsta rappers and others in the music and entertainment industries have exploited.

As children and as college students, we also were taught to pay our dues with effort, earn our rewards with work, make ourselves necessary—indeed indispensable—if we wanted to get ahead, do more than is needed before it is asked, do it well without expecting huge praise, and understand that freedom was not free. In fact, freedom brought reciprocal responsibility and demanded continuing vigilant effort. Just as we sang and were trained to "Give of Your Best to the Master" in church and chapel, so we understood that doing our best carried over into every aspect of our lives. Serving God and others well was synonymous with excellence—an internally driven ethic rather than an externally imposed requirement.

Practical adult worldly advice to youth always was grounded in a deeper message of purpose and of service reinforced by example. Education was about lifting self and about lifting others too. Unlike many of today's complaining citizens and our often spoiled children afflicted by affluenza, we were helped to put momentary setbacks in perspective. Howard Thurman's powerful reminder that "no single act or failure is ever determinative of our life" picked us up when we fell down or thought our world was coming to an end because we were jilted by a boyfriend, had flunked a course, were called a nigger by a white passerby, or had been harassed by the police for no reason other than skin color. And, for me, Dr. King's willingness to share his fears and uncertainties with us while still urging us to act in faith when we were scared encourages me still to trust God's faithfulness when faced with setbacks.

Our elders saved us from action paralysis and self-pity by putting our present problems in spiritual and historical perspective. They shared lessons of the mighty oppression of slavery, of the great dashed promises of Reconstruction, and of the violent Klan lynchings aided and abetted by powerful economic and political interests and a silent citizenry. They made us see that our individual struggles were part of an ongoing struggle for freedom and justice that had to be won over and over again and that can never be taken for granted. They also made us see that we did not have to fight these battles alone—that God was on the side of truth and righteousness, which would eventually prevail.

I do not know how I could survive the indifference

and evil and violence rife in our nation and world, and the shallowness and pettiness of so much of Washington's self-important life, without these seeds of faith, prayer, and music that were planted in my youthful soul by parents and other elders. I worry in every fiber of my being about our many children who, lacking a sense of the sacred or internal moral moorings, are trying to grow up in a society without boundaries, without respect, without enough positive role models at home, in school, in religious congregations, in our communities, in our political and economic life, and in a culture where almost anything goes on television, in the movies, in music, and in how we treat each other. Without a sense of core values like honesty, discipline, work, responsibility, perseverance, community, and service, we all become easy prey for the false idols and vultures of culturally manufactured glitz, materialism, greed, and violence. Few of us escape the suffocating vise of these things in our spiritually famished society. No value, even the Cross, has been left uncommercialized in a culture where planned obsolescence of consumer products keeps the cash registers ringing and plastic smiles, plastic cards, and plastic souls have lost touch with the genuine.

Never have we exposed children so early and relentlessly to cultural messages glamorizing violence, sex, possessions, alcohol, and tobacco with so few mediating influences from responsible adults. Never have we experienced such a numbing and reckless reliance on violence to solve problems, feel powerful, or be entertained. Never have so many children been permitted to rely on guns and gangs rather than on parents, neighbors, religious congregations, and schools for protection and guidance. Never have we pushed so many children on to the tumultuous sea of life without the life vests of nurturing families and communities, caring schools, challenged minds, job prospects, and hope.

Never before have we subjected our children to the tyranny of drugs and guns and things or taught them to look for meaning outside rather than inside themselves, teaching them in Dr. King's words "to judge success by the value of our salaries or the size of our automobiles, rather than by the quality of our service and relationships to humanity."

As we face a new century and a new millennium, the overarching challenge for America is to rebuild a sense of community and hope and civility and caring and safety for all our children. I hope God will guide our feet as parents — and guide America's feet — to reclaim our nation's soul, and to give back to all of our children their sense of security and their ability to dream about and work toward a future that is attainable and hopeful.

Let us begin by praying that God's spirit will be born anew within and among us in our own family, our extended family, and in our community, private sector, and public life. I cannot recreate the same small-town childhood of my past for my children, but I can teach and try to live the same enduring God-given and life-giving values of faith, integrity, and service. These prayers and meditations reflect my ongoing struggle to do so.

≈ I ≈

I'M YOUR CHILD

THE RITUALS OF LOVE

AND OF PARENTING

Dear God, I thank You for the gift of this child to raise, this life to share, this mind to help mold, this body to nurture, and this spirit to enrich.

Let me never betray this child's trust, dampen this child's hope, or discourage this child's dreams.

Help me dear God to help this precious child become all You mean him to be.

Let Your grace and love fall on him like gentle breezes and give him inner strength and peace and patience for the journey ahead.

God, like Hannah's son Samuel, let my children grow up in Your presence and seek out Your ways, and attend to Your work. Thank you God for my children.

❧

Oh God, help us to be worthy of the children You have entrusted to our care.

In every child who is born under no matter what circumstances and of no matter what parents, the potentiality of the human race is born again, and in him, too, once more, and each of us, our terrific responsibility toward human life: toward the utmost idea of goodness, of the horror of terrorism, and of God.

JAMES AGEE
Let Us Now Praise Famous Men

Thank You, God, for Your never-ceasing love and inexhaustible well of hope through the gift of children.

∽

O God, who loved the world so much that You gave Your only begotten Son that we might have everlasting life and who loves us so much that You gave us the gift of children, help us to be worthy of Your and their love.

∽

God, I thank You for my children.
Please be with them today in all
their coming and going and in all
their thinking and doing.

Every child comes with the message that God is not
yet discouraged of man.

RABINDRANATH TAGORE

When God wants an important thing done in this
world or a wrong righted, He goes about it in a very sin-
gular way. He doesn't release thunderbolts or stir up
earthquakes. God simply has a tiny baby born, perhaps
of a very humble home, perhaps of a very humble
mother. And God puts the idea or purpose into the
mother's heart. And she puts it in the baby's mind, and
then—God waits. The great events of this world are
not battles and elections and earthquakes and thunderbolts. The great events are babies, for each child
comes with the message that God is not yet discouraged with humanity, but is still expecting goodwill to
become incarnate in each human life.

EDMOND MCDONALD
Presbyterian Outlook

I REMEMBER vividly my fears and tears when I was twelve years old and my first niece was born prematurely after my sister developed toxemia. The baby arrived two months early by Caesarian and weighed 2 lbs. 14 ozs. How I had looked forward to her arrival! How scared I was she would not survive. How hard I prayed to God to let her live in those days before neonatal technology had advanced to its near miraculous ability today to save many of the smallest babies. How well I remember the baby Joy's great aunt Georgia, distrustful of segregated, small-town Southern medicine, insisting on taking the fragile baby under her personal wings and nursing her lovingly to health and vigor.

Since then, I have remained awed and grateful for the miracle workers who every day fight death and save life for the tiniest babies in hospital neonatal units. The fact that so many babies begin life prematurely is something we could prevent if our nation ensured cost-effective prenatal care and nutrition to every mother lacking health coverage, as many other industrialized nations do. But too many babies are born to mothers not only lacking health care but also addicted to alcohol or cocaine or infected with AIDS. My heart breaks watching these fragile little humans struggling for life! How jarring all the voices and bright lights must be after a quieter womb. How uncomfortable the many and frequent needles stuck into their bodies to feed and heal, often tearing delicate skin not yet tough enough to bear its hurtful burdens.

How I ask God to buffer the tiny little bodies and psyches and spirits against their painful entry into our world.

I cry and pray for strength and comfort for the parents who come and worry and pin notes and pray that their child will survive and be all right. And as I think back to my joyfulness at the birth of my children with all their toes, fingers, and lusty cries, how my heart goes out to parents whose child faces serious physical or mental challenges who ask themselves, Why God, why me, why my child?

And so I offer three prayers of thanks, the last one being especially for parents who are blessed and entrusted with a child with special challenges, a child equally precious and perfect in God's sight. I pray God will strengthen these families in every needed way and will surround them in the cocoon of His boundless grace.

A PREGNANT MOTHER'S PRAYER

God, I thank You for and ask Your blessing
on this child growing within me.
Keep her or him and me healthy and strong to
begin our lives together safe and sound.

O God I thank You for Your blessing of this healthy child. May she live, thrive, and strive in all Your ways.

❦

O God we thank You for this special child You have given us. By Your grace give us the special love and patience to meet her daily needs. Keep us from neglecting our other children and our own needs. Help our family share our labors together with love and understanding, and let this gift of life bring us closer together and not drive us apart.

God, help me to be honest so my children will learn
　　　honesty.
Help me to be kind so my children will learn
　　　kindness.
Help me to be faithful so my children will learn faith.
Help me to love so that my children will be loving.

☙ I BELIEVE it is an important responsibility of parents and of religious congregations—if parents choose to attend—to give their children a moral start in life. It is not the role of government to teach our children to pray.

And you shalt love the Lord your
God, with all your heart, and with all your
soul, and with all your might.

And these words which I command
you this day, teach them to your children,
and talk about them when you are at home,
when you are walking by the way, when you lie
          down,
and when you rise up. Bind them as a sign upon
your hand, and let them be a symbol between your
          eyes.
Inscribe them on the door posts of your home and on
          your gates.

Deuteronomy 6:5–9

So many children today are growing up without good work habits. Many have been spoiled or led to believe that physical labor is demeaning and that service is beneath them. Thomas Jefferson noted that slavery was a product of some not wishing to engage in manual labor. We need to teach our children that all honest work is a source of dignity and to view helping at home and in whatever setting they find themselves as expected and desirable. This is equally important for boys as well as girls. Household chores must not be seen just as mother's or sister's work. Superman needs to share responsibilities and excel at home as well as in the workplace.

Lord help me not to do for my children
what they can do for themselves.

Help me not to give them
what they can earn for themselves.

Help me not to tell them
what they can look up and find out for themselves.

Help me to help my children stand on
their own two feet and to grow into
responsible, disciplined adults.

〰 JACOB's blessing on his son Joseph and Joseph's sons Ephraim and Manasseh moves me deeply:

The God before whom my
ancestors Abraham and Isaac walked,
the God who has been my shepherd
all my life to this day,
the angel who has redeemed me
from all harm, bless the boys;
and in them let my name be perpetuated,
and the name of my ancestors Abraham and Isaac;
and let them grow into a multitude on the earth.
(Genesis 48:15–16)

My father Arthur did not live to see and bless my sons. But his life of faith and service — like my mother Maggie's — is a wellspring of blessings that my sons can draw on throughout their lives. My father often used to counsel, "Cast your bread upon the waters for you will find it after many days" (Ecclesiastes 11). His and my mother's life of devotion to their children, faith, and communities continue to guide and enrich the lives of their children and grandchildren.

O God of my father Arthur and mother Maggie, bless their children and grandchildren with Your love. Let them grow "as fruitful boughs by a spring" and may the blessings of heaven above be on their minds as they seek Your will and find Your purpose on earth.

God help me to weave a tapestry of love and not hate in my children, a spirit of tolerance and caring, and a dedication to freedom for all and not just some. God help me to sow seeds of peace and justice in my children's hearts today.

So often we wallow in our children's problems rather than exult in their strengths and possibilities. So often we dwell on the things that seem impossible rather than on the things that are possible. So often we are depressed by what remains to be done and forget to be thankful for all that has been done.

Forgive us God.

WHEN one of my children suffered an asthma attack or a painful earache or got hit in the head with a baseball, I could call or rush him to the doctor without thinking. When I hear parents talk about not being able to get help for their sick children, it makes me ashamed of our nation. How can wealthy or middle-class parents, who take their pediatrician for granted, and whose children and grandchildren might have died or suffered life-long damage if prompt health care had not been available or affordable, not demand such care for other people's children?

When children get ill, parents often feel helpless and wish they could bear their pain instead. This plea of Moses to God to heal his sister, Miriam, is a spontaneous cry from the hearts of countless parents and caregivers.

Please God, make this child well.

God, please help me not to be so busy helping other people's children that I neglect my own.

❦

God help us to shut off the television and radio and computer and phone so that we can communicate with each other. Help us to be silent like Elijah so we can hear your still, small voice within.

We take care of our possessions for our children. But of the children themselves we take not care at all. What an absurdity is this. Form the soul of Thy son aright, and all the rest will be added hereafter.

SAINT JOHN CHRYSOSTOM

Lord, let me not be so busy working to buy the things my children want that I cannot give them the time and attention and love they need.

❧

God, please help me to show my children
By my actions as well as my words
That they are loved.

PARENTING never ends. Its joys and challenges just keep changing. It's so hard to let go and let our children make their own decisions, which includes letting them make their own mistakes and living with the consequences of those mistakes. This is harder than ever today in this era of AIDS and violence when youthful mistakes can be irreparable.

Teenage and young adult years can be especially challenging for parents as we renegotiate relationships with our children, often without adequate road maps to guide us and with so little time for shared experiences when communication can flow without schedule or purpose. It is important, however, to remember that we are parents and not buddies; that it is our children's role to test parental limits but our role to set and hold to those limits and to be clear about what we really value. Even when children go against our teachings, we should lovingly—not angrily—hold onto these limits.

With the tough competition parents face from peer and media cultures, many times we lose our confidence. How to listen nonjudgmentally without abdicating our values is a struggle all parents face often. The following prayers arose out of some of my own times of anxiety and concern.

O God, please help my child to call. He doesn't know the roads are icy, he's far away, and will drive home late. I will not sleep. Please, God, protect my child.

❧

God, I was angry with my child because I was anxious. Why do I have to act that way? Why can't I be calm? Why can't I listen better?

❧

God, I said the wrong thing again and in the wrong way. Please let him know how much I love him. And please do not let my failure as a parent harm him.

❧

God, help me to say and do what needs to be said and done in the right way at the right time. Who will if I won't? I am his parent.

Oh I am who I am
The God who protected and guided
Abraham
Isaac
Jacob and
Moses

who sent Joshua to fight the battle of Jericho,
rescued Jonah from the belly of the whale to take
Your message to Nineveh,
dispatched Ezra (whose name means "help") to
proclaim Your word of law and to revive
Your people:

Protect and guide my beloved children by these
names to seek and do Your will today. Let
them always feel Your faithful presence
wherever they go and in all their
undertakings.

When they are confused, I pray they will wait for
Your clarity.

When they are afraid, I pray they will seek Your
soothing calm.

When they are alone, I pray they will feel Your loving
presence.

When they are sick, I pray You will lay Your healing
hand upon them.

When they are tired and overwrought, please lead
them to Your still waters of calm and restore
their spirits.

When they face disappointments and dashed hopes
and friends and foe alike abandon them, let
them find refuge in Your never-changing
faithfulness and love.

Oh I am who I am, I have done the best I know how
for my children. I leave the rest to You.

O God, my child is addicted to drugs and alcohol and I don't want anybody to know. Tell me what to do. Give me the strength to cope.

O God, my child has AIDS and I'm so afraid. Tell me how to help. Give me the strength to cope.

O God, my father abused me as a child and my secret eats away at me every day. Tell me where to seek help. Give me the strength to cope.

O God, my child has run away from home and I don't know where she is. Send her home and heal our rift. Give me the strength to cope.

O God, my child has joined a gang and dances with danger. Show me how to respond. Give me the strength to cope.

O God, my child is out of control. I am out of control and my life is out of control. Give me the strength to cope.

Only Your holy presence can make us well again.

LIKE many mothers of college-age or older adult children who return home during holidays and vacations, I often find myself unable to fall asleep until I hear their car in the driveway. Or if I do fall asleep, I find myself waking up periodically to check to see if my children have come home.

The mother energy that carried me through the pre-school years when there was always a child up during the night was tested again during the teenage years. We did have curfews in our home, for parental survival, during my sons' adolescent years when they began to drive and date and come home late. Now I have to depend on God's curfew!

God, please help my children to come home safely and soon so I can go to sleep. I am so tired and I have such a busy day tomorrow.

O God, go with my child as he goes to college
> Keep him safe
> Keep him sensible
> Keep him focused
> Keep him joyful
> Keep him surrounded by friends and teachers
>> who help him grow.

Help him not to succumb to alcohol or other drugs
> to the fast crowd going nowhere
> to the lure of laziness or the glamour of cliques
> to careless sex and careless habits
> but to be his own person and avoid group-think.

Help him to write more and call less!
> to know I miss him
> to feel my prayers and remember his home
>> teachings
> to visit home as often as he can and know it
>> remains a place where reservations are never
>> needed and no locks will ever bar his return.

Help him always to remember how much I love him.

᪥ As a parent, it is so hard but so necessary to let go. Our instinct is to protect even when we know we cannot.

I worry about my children every day they go about their lives of study and work and play in our unpredictable world. I alleviate my anxieties by committing their safety and guidance to God. I recall times of great danger when I believe only a mother's primal plea to God for help rescued my children: when one dashed across a busy street with an unseen car speeding around the corner; when two of my grown children, heedless of warning signs all along the beach, were nearly washed out to sea in a dangerous ocean's undertow. And I am reminded of how good God is and how dependent on Him I am and they are.

And so each day I recommit my children daily to His care. A prayer from the Hebridean Altars is one I use — inserting my children's names and those of other special people in my life in place of "me."

God be with me in this, Thy day, every day
and every way, with me and for me in this,
Thy day.

God help our children to seek and find Your words and ways, trustworthy friends and loving companions to share their days.

Guard them against the poisonous arrows of malice and violence and drugs and hate and arrogance and sloth on their journeys to adulthood.

God please keep our children on Your straight and level path.

Lord, I've raised my children and thought I was through and here I am with more.

I'm tired, I'm old, I'm broke and bent, I want to rest but can't.

My child is lost to drink and drugs, young flesh and blood needs love and care.

Lord, give me strength to do Your will and raise my grandchild well.

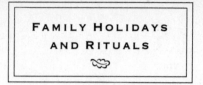

FAMILY HOLIDAYS
AND RITUALS

AFTER each of our three sons was born, we had a ceremony with family and friends to welcome them into the world, to thank God for His wondrous gifts to us, and to dedicate our lives to seeing that our children were raised in the ways of God.

Because we are a mixed religious household—I am Christian and my husband is Jewish—friends from both heritages were invited to stand with our children and serve as their godparents.

O God that knowest and lovest the hearts of children,
May they fear only Thee and walk in Thy ways, so long as they live in the land which Thou gavest unto our fathers and mothers.

Solomon's prayer
2 Chronicles 6:31

When Israel stood to receive the Torah,
The Holy One, blessed be He, said to them:
I am giving you my Torah. Bring me good guarantors
      that you will guard it, and I shall give it
      to you.
They said: Our fathers are our guarantors.
The Holy One, blessed be He, said to them:
Your fathers are unacceptable to me.
Yet bring me good guarantors, and I shall give it to
      you.
They said to him:
Master of the Universe, our prophets are our
      guarantors.
He said to them:
Your prophets are unacceptable to me.
Yet bring me good guarantors, and I shall give it to
      you.
Behold, our children are our guarantors.
The Holy One, blessed be He, said:
They are certainly good guarantors.
For their sake, I give you the Torah.

                        Jewish Midrash

꙰ UNTIL my sister Olive moved back home to South Carolina, I always cooked Thanksgiving dinner for our whole family and for friends away from their homes. Before our meal, children read various inspirational passages and this prayer of Thanksgiving. I was thrilled to find the prayer years ago and copied it from the glass case in the Howard Thurman Listening Room in Marsh Chapel at Boston University, where Thurman served as chaplain for many years. My sister later found the prayer in his book, *Meditations of the Heart.*

A PRAYER OF THANKSGIVING

Today, I make my Sacrament of Thanksgiving. I begin with the simple things of my days:

    Fresh air to breathe,
    Cool water to drink,
    The taste of food,
    The protection of houses and clothes,
    The comforts of home.

For all these I make an act of Thanksgiving this day!

I bring to mind all the warmth of humankind that I have known:

    My mother's arms,
    The strength of my father,
    The playmates of my childhood,
    The wonderful stories brought to me from the
        lives of many who talked of days gone by

when fairies and giants and all kinds of
magic held sway,
The tears I have shed, the tears I have seen,
The excitement of laughter and the twinkle in
the eye with its reminder that life is good.
For all these I make an act of Thanksgiving this day.

I finger one by one the messages of hope that awaited
me at the crossroads:
The smile of approval from those who held in
their hands the reins of my security,
The tightening of the grip in a single handshake
when I feared the step before me in the
darkness,
The whisper in my heart when the temptation
was fiercest and the claims of appetite were
not to be denied,
The crucial word said, the simple sentence from
an open page when my decision hung in the
balance.
For all these I make an act of Thanksgiving this day.

I pass before me the mainsprings of my heritage:
The fruits of the labors of countless generations
who lived before me, without whom my
own life would have no meaning,
The seers who saw visions and dreamed dreams;
The prophets who sensed a truth greater than the
mind could grasp, and whose words could
only find fulfillment in the years which they
would never see,

The workers whose sweat has watered the trees,
the leaves of which are for the healing of the
nations,

The pilgrims who set their sails for lands beyond
all horizons, whose courage made paths into
new worlds and far-off places,

The saviors whose blood was shed with a
recklessness that only a dream could inspire
and God could command.

For all these I make an act of Thanksgiving this day.

I linger over the meaning of my own life and the commitment to which I give the loyalty of my heart and
mind:

The little purposes in which I have shared with
my loves, my desires, my gifts,

The restlessness which bottoms all I do with its
stark insistence that I have never done my
best, I have never reached for the highest,

The big hope that never quite deserts me, that I
and my kind will study war no more, that
love and tenderness and all the inner graces
of Almighty affection will cover the life of
the children of God as the waters cover the
sea.

All these and more than mind can think and heart can
feel, I make as my sacrament of Thanksgiving to Thee,
Our Father, in humbleness of mind and simplicity of
heart.

God, we thank You for this food
for the hands that planted it
for the hands that tended it
for the hands that harvested it
for the hands that prepared it
for the hands that provided it
and for the hands that served it.
And we pray for those without enough food
in Your world and in our land of plenty.

Jesus, small poor baby of Bethlehem,
be born again in our hearts today
be born again in our homes today
be born again in our congregations today
be born again in our neighborhoods today
be born again in our cities today
be born again in our nations today
be born again in our world today.

Amen.

Lord I thank You for bringing all my children home for Christmas. I thank You for this time of sharing together as we celebrate Your birthday.

Lord I thank You for reminding us what life is like for the poor, for the young, and for the homeless through Your son Jesus Christ. Let us never become blind to the suffering of others.

Dear God, thank You for the gift of a new year
        to serve You
    help me to talk right
    help me to walk right
    help me to see right
    help me to feel right
    help me to do right
in Your sight.

O God of Harriet Tubman and Sojourner Truth
   of Frederick Douglass and Booker T. Washington
   of George Washington Carver and Mary McLeod
      Bethune,
Be with Your Black sons and daughters today.

O God of Martin Luther King and Malcolm X
   of James Baldwin and Fannie Lou Hamer
   of Howard Thurman and Benjamin Mays,
Be with Your Black children today.

For anyone who has experienced Black college commencements dotted by spontaneous parental shouts of "Thank You, Jesus" when their child marches across the stage to get that coveted diploma, and for all parents who struggle to get children through college, this prayer, one I found and copied after the Children's Defense Fund bought Alex Haley's farm in Clinton, Tennessee, will strike a resonant chord.

BRING THAT COLLEGE HOME

I's been sending you to college now for six or seven
          years,
Since the mornin' dat you lef' me I's been sheddin'
          bitter tears.
But I thought of dat ole sayin' "sunshine comes
          behin' de storm,"
So my young man, when you finish, you jes bring dat
          college home.

I's been scrubbin' by the washtub, I's been sweatin' in
          de fiel,
Many times I had to borry, an I almost had to steal.
But I hold on to my patience, beat dem soap suds into
          foam,
All de time my heart was sayin' he's gwine bring dat
          college home.

Folks here say you gwine be nothin', you jes foolin'
          time away,

But I shake my finger an' tell dem "wait until some
        future day."
So nex' June when dogwoods blossom and de bees
        begin to swarm,
I'll be waitin' for to see you when you bring dat
        college home.

Don't you min' dese folks here talkin', dey ain't half
        as good as you,
And deys bound to nag at good folks, dat's all dey
        know how to do.
I's got wood enough for winter, plenty clothes to keep
        me warm,
So you trot off to college, then nex' June you bring dat
        college home.

I don't mean bring home the buildings or to wreck
        dem good folks' place,
Bring home Christian education and dat high tone
        college grace.
You jes grab dem fessor's habits, hole 'em tight thru
        win' an' storm,
Den when you get your diploma, take 'em all and
        light for home.

Show dese folks dat you got 'em by the speeches dat
        you make,
By the spec's dat you'll be wearin' an' de way your
        coattail shake.

But don't git above de people, settle down, and cease
        to roam,
Be a light in your own village, be a college right here
        at home.

Anonymous poem given by Dr. Miller Boyd
of Morristown College to Alex Haley

꘎ BLACK leaders, co-convened by distinguished historian John Hope Franklin, Dorothy Height, president of the National Council of Negro Women, and myself, met in 1990 and again in 1992 for five days each at the Rockefeller Foundation conference center in Bellagio, Italy, to discuss the plight of Black children and what we could do about one of the worst crises that the Black family has faced since slavery. Agreeing that the Black community had to take the lead in addressing the crisis and in reweaving the rich fabric of community that historically fostered children's healthy development, we decided to launch the Black Community Crusade for Children (BCCC) to "leave no child behind" and to ensure every child a healthy start, a head start, a fair start, a safe start, and a moral start in life.

Each day our meetings began with a meditation and the joyful rendition of the Hallelujah Chorus from Handel's *Messiah*, from the album *A Soulful Celebration* conducted by Quincy Jones. As a result, we have endured amazingly little organizational or personal bickering as we come together to save our children.

The Reverend James Forbes, senior minister of Riverside Church in New York City, offered the following prayer, "To Set All the Children Free," during one of our meditations.

"We shall overcome" has got to be more than a frame
of mind
It's working hard in our own backyard—to leave no
child behind
"We shall overcome" has got to be more than a
children's prayer
It's sacrifice, at any price, to show them that we care

"We shall overcome" has got to be more than a
memory
It's a new resolve, to get involved in building
community
"We shall overcome" has got to be more than a
distant dream
And a place on the freedom team

"We shall overcome" has got to be more than a
protest song
It's a loving vow, to show somehow, we all can get
along
"We shall overcome" has got to be more than a
melody
It's a one-by-one till the job is done to set all the
children free

"We shall overcome" has got to be more than a
freedom song
It's confidence, being convinced that right will
conquer wrong

"We shall overcome" has got to be more than a song
         we sing
It's the will to fight, to make things right, so the
         freedom bell can ring

For the children, ring
For the children, ring

Through the power of the Spirit,
let's empower each other
to go out with power
to set all the children free.

A CHILD'S
SILENT PLEA

I PRAYED every day that God would bless me to live to see my children grow up. And I thank Him for answering my prayer. It is a deeply wrenching experience for a child to lose a parent for any reason. I still feel the sting of my daddy's death when I was fourteen and of being orphaned when I lost my mother at forty-five. Everybody needs to be someone's child — to belong to someone who will provide unconditional love that can never be taken away for any reason. I hope couples realize that having a child is a lifetime commitment and so will decide not to have children until they are ready to care for them physically, emotionally, educationally, and economically.

A CHILD'S SILENT PLEA

Mama and Daddy, *please* don't leave me,
Stay near to calm my fear.

I'm scared and lonely, hyper and ornery,
I need you, love you — please see and heed me.

Your fighting strikes terror in me,
My heart is in turmoil, my thoughts all churning.

I'm panicked and frantic and want to scream, yell,
     and shout
Don't leave me, don't leave me! Don't leave me
     behind!

Please, Mama and Daddy, I need you. I need you. I'm
     lost if you go.

I promise to . . .

Listen to my children

Communicate with my children

Teach my children right from wrong and be a good
role model for them

Spend time with and pay attention to my children

Educate my children in mind, body, and soul

Work to provide a stable family life for my children

Pray for and see God in my children and in all
children

Vote for my children to ensure them fair opportunity

Speak out for my and other people's children's needs.

❧ II ❧

SEARCH MY HEART

A STRUGGLE TOWARD
PERSONAL FAITH AND COURAGE

FAITH

God supports me now
God guides me now
God loves me now
All is well with me now.

Our Father and Mother who art in Heaven, let Your will and not mine be done. Hallowed be Your name and not mine on earth and in Heaven. Give me this day my daily bread and help me not to worry about tomorrow. Forgive me my sins and give me a spirit of forgiveness for the sins of others. Lead me away from temptation and trouble and deliver me from my own evil and that of others. And keep my eyes not on the world's fleeting power and glory today but on Your Kingdom, Your power, and Your glory forever.

O God, let fear die and conviction be born in our
          lives.
Let Your light dawn in our minds as the day dawns
          on the earth.
Let us not be so busy hurrying into the future and
          worrying about the past that we lose
          today—the only one we have.
God, help us do what we know we have to do today,
          and leave tomorrow to You.

O God, help me to realize that now is a part of timeless
time—of eternity. Help me to know that I am one
with You and that Your presence is here and now and
forever.

Dear God, help me always to give You the right-of-way
in my life.

Somebody's knocking at your door,
Somebody's knocking at your door,
O children, why don't you answer?
Somebody's knocking at your door.

Knocks like Jesus, somebody's knocking at your door,
Can't you hear Him, somebody's knocking at your
        door,
Jesus calls you, somebody's knocking at your door.

                                        Negro spiritual

Lord, help us to hear when You knock.

Lord, You told us we cannot serve You and wealth. Help me to choose You.

Lord, You told us not to worry about our lives or drink or bodies or clothes. Help us to seek Your will, do Your work, and trust You to provide.

Lord, You told us not to worry about tomorrow, which brings worries of its own. Help us to live right now for You.

Lord, help me to spend as much time making sure the world doesn't change me as I spend trying to change the world.

I SAY this prayer every morning when I rise. It connects me to the singing in my childhood church and helps me try to submit my will to God daily.

> Lord, I want to go where You want me to go
> Do what You want me to do
> Be what You want me to be
> Save me!

Negro spiritual

O God, help me to feel Your presence everywhere I go today.

To see You in everyone I meet today.

To sense You in all I hear today.

To reflect You in all I do today.

To pray to and trust You in all I experience today.

To struggle to be like You in all I am today.

To speak of and for You in all I say today.

To thank You for everything every day.

O God, whose awesome deeds turned the sea into dry land for the Israelites to cross to freedom and transformed rocky hillsides into seas of wildflowers nourished by hidden streams, our spirits cry out in thankful praise for Your wondrous abundance of life.

Just to be is a blessing. Just to live is holy.

RABBI ABRAHAM HESCHEL
I Asked for Wonder

O God, by faith, like Abraham, let us obey Your call to leave our comfortable homes and set out for strange places although we do not know for certain where we are going.

By faith, like Noah, let us heed Your signs and warnings and build sturdy arks to rescue our children from the coming floods.

By faith, like Isaac and Jacob, let us seek Your blessings on our children's futures.

By faith, like Moses, let us leave Pharaoh's house and head across the wilderness to lead our oppressed children to freedom.

By faith, like Joseph, let us turn evil into good and welcome our erring brothers and kin with a spirit of reconciliation and love.

By faith, like the child David, let us go out without fear to face the Goliaths of our day with slingshots of righteousness and justice confident of Your divine guidance and protection.

COMMITMENT

Help me to dedicate each hour of each day to You—
my constant, never-failing companion and guide.

God, please give me the courage of my conviction
        this day.
Help me not to waver.
Help me not to procrastinate.
Help me not to rationalize.
Help me not to play games with myself.
Help me to stand strong with Thee.

Lord, help me not just to give what I have but to give
what I am.

Lord, think Your thoughts in me
do Your work through me
build Your peace in me
share Your love through me.

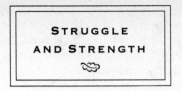

STRUGGLE
AND STRENGTH

I just want to cry and cry and cry, Lord,
I can't bear my burden today or see my way
to tomorrow.

≈ CHURCH folk often sing that God may not come when you ask Him but He always comes on time. Sometimes I sure wish He would hurry up because I don't think I can hold on for another minute or get up to fight another day.

> Lord, please help me to hang on.
> Please don't let me give up.
> Help me to remember that,
> like the sun in the morning,
> You come when it is time.

O Lord, help me to understand that you ain't going to let nothing come my way that You and me together can't handle.

Anonymous African boy

Lord, straighten my back
   clear my head
   strengthen my voice
   infuse my heart
   with Your mighty spirit.

God, help us to be like bamboo, which bends and bows and sways in the winds of change but never breaks.

☙ THIS is a prayer of a Negro boy running a race:

Lord, You pick 'em up and I'll put 'em down,
You pick 'em up and I'll put 'em down.

☙

Lord, if You have to break me to remake me, let Your
will be done.

GUIDANCE

Lord, I'm completely lost and have gone to look for myself.

Please help me to wait until I can find me—and Thee—again.

Lord, who am I?
Am I what You want me to be?

Lord, what do I want?
Is it what You want me to want?

What and in whom do I believe?
Is it You?

Thomas Merton's wonderful prayer captures my frequent despair when I wonder what in the world I'm doing and whether it adds up to anything. In this time of fickle fads, citizen confusion, and seething anger, I have turned to Merton's prayer again and again as I've asked for guidance.

THE ROAD AHEAD

My Lord God, I have no idea where I am going. I do not see the road ahead of me. I cannot know for certain where it will end. Nor do I really know myself, and the fact that I think I am following your will does not mean that I am actually doing so. But I believe that the desire to please you does in fact please you. And I hope I have that desire in all that I am doing. I hope that I will never do anything apart from that desire. And I know that if I do this you will lead me by the right road, though I may know nothing about it. Therefore I will trust you always though I may seem to be lost and in the shadow of death. I will not fear, for you are ever with me, and you will never leave me to face my perils alone.

Lord, replace my blindness with Your vision
My deafness with Your healing voice
My insensitivity with Your understanding
My sinfulness with Your love.

Lord, help me to persist although I want to give up.
Lord, help me to keep trying although I can't see
          what good it does.
Lord, help me to keep praying although I'm not sure
          You hear me.
Lord, help me to keep living in ways that seek to
          please You.

Lord, help me to know when to lead and when to
          follow.
Lord, help me to know when to speak and when to
          remain silent.
Lord, help me to know when to act and when to wait.

Lord, give me good sense and a good spirit today. I am sorely lacking in both. Only You can help me overcome me.

❧

Lord, I want to be free of the pressure to do great things in the world by being great in doing small things for Thee.

PATIENCE

God, I am scurrying around like a chicken with her head cut off, making a mess everywhere I light.

Why, God, when I know if I wait quietly and listen for Your guidance, I do better and work more efficiently, do I rush about — driven by time, rather than by You?

Help me, God, to slow down, to be silent, so I can hear You and do Your will and not mine.

Lord, help me not to try to do everything myself or act as if only I can do it right. Help me to empower others and respect their right to do it their way and at their own pace. Lord, teach me patience.

Lord, help me to sort out what I should do first, second, and third today and to not try to do everything at once and nothing well. Give me the wisdom to delegate what I can and to order the things I can't delegate, to say no when I need to, and the sense to know when to go home.

O Lord, there is too much Martha in me today and not enough Mary. Help me to sit down at your feet and listen.

Lord, help me to slow down and see the extraordinary miracles in the ordinary things of every day's existence.

FORGIVENESS

Lord, I cannot believe I thought what I thought, said what I said, or did what I did. I cannot believe the meanness of my spirit and the impatience of my manner. I don't want to be like this, Lord. By Thy grace, please change me.

O God, help me to be real and not pretend to be what I'm not or to know what I don't. Help me not to be despairing or prideful in comparing myself to others when I cannot measure up or think they don't. You did not teach us to compete but to cooperate and love.

O God, forgive my unkind words, my harsh tone, my impatient gesture, my ruthless perfectionism. Like the Apostle Paul, "I do not do the good I want, but the evil I do not want is what I do." Please infuse my weak sinful self with Thy gentle loving spirit.

O God, help me today to be happy and helpful rather than irritable and critical, to get myself out of the way so that others can sense You and not me.

Help me not to waste time worrying about the bad world we have but to use the time I have working for the better world our children need.

≈ I A M as mad and sad as Heaven must be when children are killed and adults are silent. I am as awed and humbled as Hell must be by the courage of those who carry on after unfathomable loss with love as this Iranian father did. I have seen this same generous spirit among many of the hundreds of families who have lost children to senseless gun violence — who seek some meaning for their loss by working to stop the violence against other children. I hope this father's moving prayer of reconciliation will help all parents struggling with such loss. It is shameful that the morally unthinkable has become normal as a child is killed by guns every two hours in America.

A FATHER'S PRAYER
UPON THE MURDER OF HIS SON

O God,
We remember not only our son but also his
       murderers;
Not because they killed him in the prime of his
       youth and made our hearts bleed and our
       tears flow;
Not because with this savage act they have brought
       further disgrace on the name of our country
       among the civilized nations of the world;
But because through their crime we now follow Your
       footsteps more closely in the way of
       sacrifice.

The terrible fire of this calamity burns up all
      selfishness and possessiveness in us;
Its flame reveals the depth of depravity and meanness
      and suspicion, the dimension of hatred and
      the measure of sinfulness in human nature;
It makes obvious as never before our need to trust in
      God's love as shown in the cross of Jesus and
      his resurrection;
Love which makes us free from hate toward our
      persecutors;
Love which brings patience, forbearance, courage,
      loyalty, humility, generosity, greatness of
      heart;
Love which more than ever deepens our trust in
      God's final victory and his eternal designs
      for the Church and for the world;
Love which teaches us how to prepare ourselves to
      face our own day of death.
O God,
Our son's blood has multiplied the fruit of the Spirit
      in the soil of our souls;
So when his murderers stand before You on the day of
      judgment
Remember the fruit of the Spirit by which they have
      enriched our lives.
And Forgive.

BISHOP DEHQANI-TAFTI OF IRAN

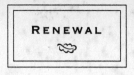

RENEWAL

Lord, unwrinkle my tired soul
    unsnarl my garbled thoughts and words
    unwind my gnarled nerves
    and let me relax in Thee.

Lord, I am so tired of climbing mountain after mountain. I want to sit down right here and rest.

❧

Lord, help me to keep moving ahead when I want to give up and turn back. Help me to put one foot in front of the other to get over this new mountain You've given me to climb on the way home to You.

SOMETIMES I just have to flee schedules and expectations (mostly self-imposed) and try to get quiet enough within to remember that God is in charge of my life and of the world — not I. My sinful sense of indispensability slowly drops away as I sink into a cushion of silence, hospitality, and worship with the nuns of All Saints Convent in Catonville, Maryland, or in retreat elsewhere. I share here a prayer I found at All Saints that helps me overcome the useless burdens of self-importance and excessive busyness.

THE NUNS' TWENTY-THIRD PSALM

The Lord is my pace-setter, I shall not rush.
He makes me stop and rest for quiet intervals;
He provides me with images of stillness, which
        restore my serenity.
He leads me in ways of efficiency through calmness
        of mind.
And His guidance is peace.
Even though I have a great many things to
        accomplish each day,
I will not fret, for His presence is here.
His timelessness, his all-importance will keep me in
        balance.
He prepares refreshment and renewal in the midst of
        my activity
By anointing my mind with His oils of tranquility.

My cup of joyous energy overflows.
Surely harmony and effectiveness shall be the fruit of
　　　my hours for
I shall walk in the place of my Lord and dwell in His
　　　House forever.

O God, whose love is as everlasting as the ocean's roar and as ceaseless as the tide's to and fro, wash away the daily flotsam of cares with Your refreshing grace.

❧

Lord, I am running on empty and need You to fill me
        up so I can keep going.
My weary spirit needs to lie fallow and wait for You
        to prepare its soil for planting again.
My overtaxed mind is tired of racing to keep up with
        the speeding treadmill of purposeless
        politics going nowhere.
I need to rest and withdraw, to think, and to resist the
        presumptuous temptation of thinking that it
        is I and not You who must build the national
        house of decency for our children.
Lord, I thank You for this time of rest.

THANKS

Thank You God for the rain which grows the trees
　　　　and makes the leaves green.
Thank You God for Your Spirit which grows the will
　　　　and makes the soul strong.
Thank You God for everything.

In the middle of winter the buds prepare for spring.
Thank you God for unceasing life.

The dull, brown stalks of spent hydrangeas mirror my spent spirit. Yet green and blue and pink colors dance in my mind's eye for the spring within and without about to come.

I feel your presence in pealing cathedral bells, in insistent cawing crows, in intricate yellow petals of January forsythia, in new growth heralding coming spring.

Thank You God for hope.

O God, I thank You for this day of life
for eyes to see the sky
for ears to hear the birds
for feet to walk amidst the trees
for hands to pick the flowers from the earth
for a sense of smell to breathe in the sweet perfumes
of nature
for a mind to think about and appreciate the magic of
everyday miracles
for a spirit to swell in joy at Your mighty presence
everywhere.

O God of the blue, red, brown, black, and multicolored bird, of the singing, humming, and silent bird, of the noisy woodpecker and the cooing dove, of perfect yellow sunflowers, fanciful laughing pansies, and pungent purple lavender, thank You for Your beautiful gifts of rich difference and variety.

O God, whose countless shades of green we cannot discern, who made no two leaves, grasses, animals, or humans alike, who made blue sky, white and gray clouds, soft reddish-brown and black earthen soils, infinite desert sands and impenetrable oceans deep, we thank You for the manifold and diverse universe You have made and shared with us.

※ III ※

STAND BY ME

ON JUSTICE

FOR CHILDREN

ᗏᗏ ON a walk through Harvard Square one day, after my family had moved to the Boston area where the Children's Defense Fund (CDF) had its beginning in a wonderful old clapboard house in Cambridge, I saw in a shop window this charming drawing by a child named Maria Coté. I immediately bought it.

In 1974, when the Children's Defense Fund completed its first report, *Children Out of School in America*, I asked permission from Maria's mother to use the drawing on the cover. Although I later learned that the prayer was attributed to Breton and to Swedish fishermen, the child's depiction of the prayer is what gave it special meaning for me.

A few years after the Children's Defense Fund began, someone suggested we ought to have a logo. I asked a graphic arts firm to develop one. Not liking what they did, I looked at Maria's drawing above my desk and realized it reflected the Children's Defense Fund's mission more truthfully than any abstract drawing could. Maria's mother agreed to our trademarking her daughter's drawing.

Maria was five years old when she drew this picture. I was thrilled to run into her again in 1989 when my son Joshua graduated from Harvard, where Maria worked in the president's office. I later sent her CDF's poster with her logo, which has been reprinted hundreds of thousands of times. Recently, she recounted that her parents—both of whom are artists—had their five children draw pictures for a homemade calendar to be assembled as a Christmas gift for a family friend. Maria's mother had given her the fisherman's prayer and told her to draw what it symbolized to her. Her mother liked the drawing so much that she asked Maria to draw another one and kept our "logo" herself. An artist friend of her mother's had it displayed in his Harvard Square gallery near my office, where I saw it.

I recently heard that a variation of this fisherman's prayer, without Maria's special touch, had been in the Oval Office during both President Kennedy's and President Carter's White House years, and I understand that Admiral Hyman Rickover used to give a plaque with the prayer to the skipper of every new Polaris submarine. His Navy version says, "O God, Thy sea is so great, and my boat is so small."

There have been many days working for children since I first saw Maria's drawing when I've felt buffeted by the tidal waves of callous politics and greed. Children's tiny lifeboats are so often caught up in the choppy ocean waters of politics and are smashed by political tidal waves or submerged in their wake and left to bob to shore alone by the huge ocean liners of special interests. I feel so frustrated as relatively small immunization and Head Start and child health and nutrition and child care investments are rolled into big, complicated budget reconciliation bills — rushed along on political currents that can drown or jettison them at any moment. When I despair and feel powerless to get our nation to feed and house and protect children, I remind myself of the significant progress made for children since CDF's work began. For example, the *Education for all Handicapped Children's Act*, passed in 1974, resulted in millions of handicapped children going to school and becoming more productive rather than dependent adults. Thanks to the successful Head Start program and a new child care law, millions of children have been kept safe and prepared for school and have become a part of mainstream society. During the '60s and '70s, child hunger was largely eliminated and infant mortality rates decreased significantly. Yet we have such a long way to go.

Why is there still, in post–Cold War America, such unbearable dissonance between promise and performance; between good politics and good policy; between America's racial creed and America's racial deed; between professed and practiced family values; between calls for community and rampant individualism and greed; between our capacity to prevent and alleviate child killing, poverty, and disease and our political and spiritual will to do so in the richest and most powerful nation on earth?

Every time regressive politics seek to cut away the still inadequate national safety net for children, I determine to build a bigger and safer boat with stronger oars to survive stormy political waters, in order that our great nation will leave no child behind.

Lord, we have pushed so many of our children into the tumultuous sea of life in leaky boats without survival gear.

Forgive us and help them to forgive us. Help us now to give all our children the anchor of faith, the rudder of hope, the sails of education, and the paddles of family to keep them going when life's sea gets rough.

O God, forgive our rich nation where small babies die of cold quite legally.

O God, forgive our rich nation where small children suffer from hunger quite legally.

O God, forgive our rich nation where toddlers and school children die from guns sold quite legally.

O God, forgive our rich nation that lets children be the poorest group of citizens quite legally.

O God, forgive our rich nation that lets the rich continue to get more at the expense of the poor quite legally.

O God, forgive our rich nation which thinks security rests in missiles rather than in mothers, and in bombs rather than in babies.

O God, forgive our rich nation for not giving You sufficient thanks by giving to others their daily bread.

O God, help us never to confuse what is quite legal with what is just and right in Your sight.

Better the occasional faults of a government that lives in a spirit of charity than the constant omissions of a government frozen in the ice of its own indifference.

FRANKLIN D. ROOSEVELT

Lord, You told us, "Blessed are the poor in spirit."
The world says, "Blessed are those high on spirits."

You said, "Blessed are those who mourn."
The world says, "Blessed are those who maim and
torture."

You said, "Blessed are the meek."
The world says, "Blessed are the arrogant and the
strong."

You said, "Blessed are those who hunger and thirst
for righteousness."
The world says, "Blessed are those who hunger and
thirst for fleeting power and fame."

You said, "Blessed are the merciful."
The world says, "Blessed are the mercenary and
punitive."

You said, "Blessed are the pure in heart."
The world says, "Blessed are the hard of heart."

You said, "Blessed are the peacemakers."
The world says, "Blessed are the weaponmakers."

You said, "Blessed are those who are persecuted for
righteousness' sake."
The world says, "Blessed are those who persecute for
the sake of riches and race."

You said, "Blessed are you when people revile you
　　　　　and persecute you and utter all kinds of evil
　　　　　about you falsely on my account."
The world says, "Blessed are you when people
　　　　　applaud you and praise you for your own
　　　　　sake."

Help us, Lord, to find our way to You.

God, please stop injustice,
the killing of innocent children
by violence at home and in faraway lands.

God, please stop injustice,
the killing of innocent children
by poverty at home and abroad.

God, please stop injustice,
the killing of innocent child spirits
by vanity and greed in our land and others.

God, please stop injustice,
the assault on precious child dreams
by neglect and apathy near and far.

God, please stop injustice,
so our children may live
and love and laugh and play again.

But the child's sob in the silence curses deeper than the strong man in his wrath.

ELIZABETH BARRETT BROWNING

ALL during the Christmas season, as millions celebrate a poor, homeless child Christians call Savior, I think about the irony of some political leaders proposing (and citizens permitting) policies that would result in millions more children becoming destitute, homeless, and hungry, and even being placed in orphanages away from their parents. Herod is riding across our land again.

Lord help us.

Lord, it is Christmas and
Herod is searching for and destroying our children,
pillaging their houses, corrupting their minds,
killing and imprisoning the sons, orphaning the
            daughters,
widowing the mothers.

Herod's soldiers are everywhere,
in government, on Wall Street, in the church
            house, schoolhouse, and moviehouse,

Lead us and our children to safety.

God, we confess that ours is still a world in which
        Herod seems to rule:
    the powerful are revered,
    the visions of the wise are ignored,
    the poor are afflicted,
    and the innocent are killed.

You show us that salvation comes
in the vulnerability of a child,
yet we hunger for the "security" of weapons and
        walls.

You teach us that freedom comes in loving service,
yet we trample on others in our efforts to be "free."

Forgive us, God, when we look to the palace
instead of the stable,
when we heed politicians more than prophets.

Renew us with the spirit of Bethlehem,
That we may be better prepared for Your coming.

Amen.

From *Thankful Praise:*
A Resource for Christian Worship,
edited by Keith Watkins

God, You send us Your prophets and we ignore or kill
    them.
You send us Your children and we neglect and abuse
    them.
You send us Your Son, whom we worship and adore
    but fail to follow.
God have mercy on us sinners.

God, is America's dream big enough for me?
For the little Black boy born the wrong color in the
            wrong place
to the wrong parents in some folks' sight?

God, is America's justice fair enough for me?
For the little Brown or White girl labelled from birth
            as second best?

God, is America's economy open to us?
For the many children who have to stay poor on the
            bottom so too few
can stay rich on the top?

God, does America have enough for me in a land of
            plenty for some,
but of famine for others?

God, is America's dream large enough for me?
I who am poor, average, disabled, girl, Black, Brown,
            Native American, White?

Is America for me?

⁓ I KEEP the Eight Degrees of Tsedakah on my refrigerator to remind me and my family to share what we have with others — joyfully and without a lot of fanfare — and to think about what and how to give effectively.

According to Jewish law, reaching out to the needy and doing so in a manner that prevents the needy person's requiring charity — by helping them help themselves through jobs or interest-free loans — is encouraged. I believe that both our private charity and public policies should reach out to protect children from want by ensuring their parents jobs and the tools of work — training, child care, health care — and by making sure their children get a healthy start in life to prevent future dependency.

Charity also is something we should engage in to respond to immediate and emergency needs. But charity is no substitute for justice, and fair opportunity must exist for every child if a fair chance for all Americans is to result.

There are eight degrees in the giving of tsedakah, one higher than the other.

1. Those who give grudgingly, reluctantly, or with regret.
2. Those who give less than is fitting, but give graciously.
3. Those who give what is fitting, but only after being asked.
4. Those who give before being asked.
5. Those who give without knowing to whom, although the recipients know the identity of the donors.
6. Those who give without making their identity known to the recipients.
7. Those who give without knowing to whom, and neither do the recipients know from whom they receive.
8. Those who help others by giving a gift or loan, or by making them business partners or finding them employment, thereby helping them dispense aid to others. As Scripture says, "You shall strengthen him, be he a stranger or a settler, he shall live with you" (Leviticus 23:35). This means strengthening them in such a manner that falling into want is prevented.

An epitome of Maimonides' Eight Degrees of Tsedakah;
Mishnah Torah, Gifts to the Needy, 10

Lord, we fear our children whose young fears we
could not allay and whose lives we do not
protect.
Lord, we cry for our children whose tears we did not
wipe and whose spirits have been frozen by
the cold indifference of unfriendly
communities.
Lord, turn our and their despair into daring action,
turn our and their pain into renewed purpose,
turn our and their confusion into caring and
commitment,
turn our and their disappointments into
determination and love,
turn our and their fears into the fight for right.

Lord, baptize us with Your holy spirit and fire so that
we may light a mighty flame of justice in all the land.

O God, in this America where values seem to change every day like fads and fashion and MTV, help me cling to You who changes not.

O God, in this America where so few have so much and so many have so little, help me to keep faith with the poor and young.

O God, in this America where politicians attempt to overrule the prophets, and pundits arrogantly disparage the gospel, help me to speak straight and strong.

O GOD OF ALL CHILDREN

O God of the children of Somalia, Sarajevo, South
      Africa, and South Carolina
Of Albania, Alabama, Bosnia, and Boston,
Of Cracow and Cairo, Chicago and Croatia,
Help us to love and respect and protect them all.

O God of Black and Brown and White and Albino
      children and those all mixed together,
Of children who are rich and poor and in between,
Of children who speak English and Spanish and
      Russian and Hmong and languages our ears
      cannot discern,
Help us to love and respect and protect them all.

O God of the child prodigy and the child prostitute,
      of the child of rapture and the child of rape,
Of runaway or thrown-away children who struggle
      every day without parent or place or friend
      or future,
Help us to love and respect and protect them all.

O God of children who can walk and talk and hear
and see and sing and dance and jump and
play and of children who wish they could
but can't,
Of children who are loved and unloved, wanted and
unwanted,
Help us to love and respect and protect them all.

O God of beggar, beaten, abused, neglected,
homeless, AIDS, drug, and hunger-ravaged
children,
Of children who are emotionally and physically and
mentally fragile,
and of children who rebel and ridicule, torment and
taunt,
Help us to love and respect and protect them all.

O God of children of destiny and of despair, of war
and of peace,
Of disfigured, diseased, and dying children,
Of children without hope and of children with hope
to spare and to share,
Help us to love and respect and protect them all.

I BELIEVE that hope is one of the best contraceptives to teen pregnancy and one of the best antidotes to violence. Children need to have a sense of an achievable future in order to make good choices. They also need good choices and families, communities, and a nation that value and protect them enough to give them the time, attention, and necessities they need to succeed. Parents are the most important people in the lives of children, but parents need jobs and the support of their community to fulfill their responsibilities to their families.

> Lord, our children are having children
> and we don't know what to do.
>
> Lord, our children are killing children
> and we don't know what to do.
>
> Help us, Lord, to hear their cries.
> Tell us what to do.

Lord, help us to plant our children like trees by streams of water so that they will yield full fruit in their season.

Lord, help our children to prosper in all their ways and not wither on the vine of our parched streets, barren rural fields, anemic spiritual lives, and materialistic culture.

∽

A CHILD LOST

A child drowned today,
dreams, hopes, laughter, all gone
without a peep in the muddy lake.

A child died today
helpless, unheard, lost on the
mean streets of the U.S.A.

A child was killed today,
tender baby life snuffed out
by bomb blasts of random hate.

God please have mercy on their souls
and ours.

〰 I FIRST heard Ina Hughes's wonderful prayer for children at a meeting of state chief school officers in Montana. The reader was Craig Phillips, then state superintendent of education in North Carolina, who used it to introduce me to the group. I have never experienced a better introduction. This prayer movingly captures the inextricable link between loving and caring for our own children and other people's children with whom we and our children must share our communities and nation.

We pray/accept responsibility for children
   who sneak Popsicles before supper,
   who erase holes in math workbooks,
   who can never find their shoes.

And we pray/accept responsibility for those
   who stare at photographers from behind barbed
         wire,
   who can't bound down the street in a new pair of
         sneakers,
   who never "counted potatoes,"
   who were born in places we wouldn't be caught
         dead,
   who never go to the circus,
   who live in an X-rated world.

We pray/accept responsibility for children
    who bring us sticky kisses and fistfuls of
        dandelions,
    who hug us in a hurry and forget their lunch
        money.

And we pray/accept responsibility for those
    who never get dessert,
    who have no safe blanket to drag behind them,
    who watch their parents watch them die,
    who can't find any bread to steal,
    who don't have any rooms to clean up,
    whose pictures aren't on anybody's dresser,
    and whose monsters are real.

We pray/accept responsibility for children
    who spend all their allowance before Tuesday,
    who throw tantrums in the grocery store and pick
        at their food,
    who like ghost stories,
    who shove dirty clothes under the bed and never
        rinse out the tub,
    who get visits from the tooth fairy,
    who don't like to be kissed in front of the carpool,
    who squirm in church or temple and scream in the
        phone,
    whose tears we sometimes laugh at and whose
        smiles can make us cry.

And we pray/accept responsibility for those
   whose nightmares come in the daytime,
   who will eat anything,
   who have never seen a dentist,
   who aren't spoiled by anybody,
   who go to bed hungry and cry themselves to sleep,
   who live and move, but have no being.

We pray/accept responsibility for children
   who want to be carried and for those who must,
   for those we never give up on and for those
   who don't get a second chance,
   for those we smother and for those who will grab
         the hand of anyone kind enough to offer it.

(Adapted from Ina J. Hughes)

God, help us to remember that every child is a gift from You for whom You have a special and unwavering love. Just as You can love the hell out of us, help us to love the hell out of children many of us are eager to write off as lost and to give up on as hopeless.

God, help us to remember
that there are no
illegitimate children in Your sight.

꒰꒱ S o much of America's tragic and costly failure to care for all its children stems from our tendency to distinguish between our own children and other people's children — as if justice were divisible. The pervasive breakdown of moral, family, and community values, and the widespread presence of drugs, violence, teen pregnancy, neglect, and abuse in every race and income group should help us realize our common interest in investing in and protecting all children — other people's as well as our own.

An African proverb reminds us that the rain falls on all the village huts and not just on some. So it is with violence and drugs and family and cultural decay today. All of us are affected by other people's children, in the fears we harbor, the taxes we pay, the prisons we build, the welfare we love to hate, and in the nagging sense that we are not living up to our professed values of fair opportunity for all.

O God, we pray for our children and family members and for our neighbors' children. Help us God to remember that all Your people are our neighbors and all their children are our own.

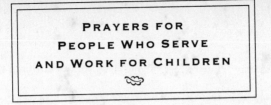

PRAYERS FOR
PEOPLE WHO SERVE
AND WORK FOR CHILDREN

Lord, I want to be ready to struggle just like Medgar
in Jackson
To walk just like King in Memphis and Chicago
To speak truth to power everywhere just like
Sojourner and Douglass
To march on Washington like Randolph and Lewis
To walk in Jerusalem with You.

O God, help us to recover our hope for our children's
      sake.

Help us to recover our courage for our children's sake.

Help us to recover our discipline for our children's
      sake.

Help us to recover our ability to work together for
      our children's sake.

Help us to recover our values for our children's sake.

Help us to recover a spirit of sacrifice for our
      children's sake.

Help us to recover our faith in Thee for our children's
      sake.

Dear God, I do not know how to help the forty-year-old alcoholic sleeping in the Brooklyn subway. But tell me how to save his child.

God, I don't know what to say to that mother who has lost her only child to violence. But help me save other parents from that pain.

I don't know how to light the dimmed eyes of the crack-addicted mother who has abandoned her child for a moment's escape from the cruel world. But, God, show me how to salvage her child.

Everybody can be great. Because anybody can serve. You don't have to have a college degree to serve. You don't have to make your subject and your verb agree to serve. You don't have to know about Plato and Aristotle to serve. You don't have to know Einstein's theory of relativity to serve. You don't have to know the second theory of thermodynamics in physics to serve. You only need a heart full of grace. A soul generated by love.

DR. MARTIN LUTHER KING, JR.

Lord, forgive us for making excuses, complaining, and doing nothing.
Help us to realize that there is never any unemployment or underemployment if we truly seek to serve You.

〰️ THIS wonderful prayer reminds us that so many good people work so hard every day all over our land and world to help those in need — acting as God's hands and feet and ears and voice. They give me nourishment to keep going. I thank God for people who care, and I pray that God will send many more laborers to increase our children's harvest.

IN PRAISE OF HANDS

Blessed be the works of Your hands,
O Holy One.
Blessed be these hands that have touched life.
Blessed be these hands that have nurtured creativity.
Blessed be these hands that have held pain.
Blessed be these hands that have embraced with
          passion.
Blessed be these hands that have tended gardens.
Blessed be these hands that have closed in anger.
Blessed be these hands that have planted new seeds.
Blessed be these hands that have harvested ripe fields.
Blessed be these hands that have cleaned, washed,
          mopped, scrubbed.
Blessed be these hands that have become knotty with
          age.
Blessed be these hands that are wrinkled and scarred
          from doing justice.

Blessed be these hands that have reached out and
            been received.
Blessed be these hands that hold the promise of the
            future.
Blessed be the works of Your hands,
O Holy One.

DIANN L. NEU

Lord, help us to spend less time on what we need to have and more time on who we need to be and what we need to do as Your hands and feet and voice of mercy and justice in the world.

Lord, please let our small mustard seeds of daily service grow into great shrubs of change and trees in whose branches the birds can nest and in whose shade our children can rest and feel safe.

Lord, help me not to be a taker but a tender,
Lord, help me not to be a whiner but a worker,
Lord, help me not to be a getter but a giver,
Lord, help me not to be a hindrance but a help,
Lord, help me not to be a critic but a catalyst
        for good.

did not call us to succeed,
called us to serve.

did not call us to win,
God called us to work.

God did not call us to live long,
God called us to live for Him.

God did not call us to be happy,
God called us to be hopeful.

God did not call us to fame,
God called us to faith.

God did not call us to seek power,
God called us to seek peace.

God did not call us to loot the earth and each other,
God called us to love our earth and each other.

◦≈◦

O God, take our tiny acorns of service and turn them
into towering oak trees of hope.

ॐ BEFORE every speech I make, I silently ask God to bless the saying and to bless the hearing of the words I share about our children's needs to His service and glory.

O God, help me to say what You want me to say and how You want me to say it.

We thank you, God, for this time of change, challenge, struggle, learning, witness, and action for and with our children. Thou counseled us to "take care that we not despair" and that it is not the will of our Father in Heaven that even "one of these little ones be lost."

Help us, God, to overcome our selfishness and greed, our political and personal jockeying, our individual and organizational agendas, our need to be first, right, and recognized, and to become humble like the child whom Christ said is the "greatest in the Kingdom of Heaven."

Then they came to Capernaum; and when he was in the house he asked them, "What were you arguing about on the way?" But they were silent, for on the way they had argued with one another who was the greatest. He sat down, called the twelve, and said to them, "Whoever wants to be first must be last of all and servant of all." Then he took a little child and put it among them; and taking it in his arms, he said to them, "Whoever welcomes one such child in my name welcomes me, and whoever welcomes me welcomes not me but the one who sent me."

Mark 9:33–37

Thank You

for work
   which engages me in an internal debate
      between right and reward
   and stretches me toward responsibility
   to those who pay for my work,
      and those who cannot pay
         because they have no work;

for justice
   which repairs the devastations of poverty;

for liberty
   which extends to the captives of violence;

for healing
   which binds up the broken-bodied
   and the broken-hearted;

for bread broken
   for all the hungry earth;

for good news
   of love which is stronger than death;

and for peace
        for all to sit under fig trees
              and not be afraid;

for my calling . . . my life.

TED LODER

So often we want to see immediately the results of what we do. But Leo Tolstoy and Reinhold Niebuhr remind us that our most important acts are often unforeseeable and unforeseen.

> The most important acts, both for the one who accomplishes them and for his fellow creatures, are those that have remote consequences.
>
> LEO TOLSTOY

> Nothing that is worth doing can be achieved in our lifetime; therefore we must be saved by hope. Nothing which is true and beautiful or good makes complete sense in any immediate context of history; therefore we must be saved by faith. Nothing we do, however virtuous, can be accomplished alone; therefore we are saved by love. No virtuous act is quite as virtuous from the standpoint of our friend or foe as it is from our standpoint; therefore we must be saved by the final form of love which is forgiveness.
>
> REINHOLD NIEBUHR
> *The Irony of American History*, 1952

O God, help us try to do the right thing and leave the right results to You. Help us to plant and water and nourish as many seeds of hope and love and care as we can, even if we do not see them flower or will not know what harvest they will yield. Help us like Job to be able to say, "I have always acted justly and fairly. I was eyes for the blind and feet for the lame. I was like a father and mother to the poor and took the side of strangers in trouble. I destroyed the power of cruel men and rescued their victims."

God, guide our faith that by it we might make our children and nation whole again.

God, help us to believe with every ounce of our being that we, with Your help, can save our children and make them well, as you did the woman who said, "If I can only touch His cloak!"

God, renew our spirits — Your spirit within us — and make us worthy carriers of Your message of love and hope and life in all we say and do this day and forever more.

Lord, let us exile defeat
    wrestle despair to the floor
    throw apathy to the winds
    and feed depression to the hogs.

Lord, help us to stand up and fight for our children.

God, protect us from and keep us from being
>Hypocrites
>Experts
>Attention huggers
>Blamers and complainers
>Snake oil salespeople
>Takers and just talkers
>Lone Rangers
>Excuse makers
>Fair weather workers
>Braggers
>Magic bullet seekers and sellers and
>Quitters.

God, send us and help us to be
>Righteous warriors
>Moral guerrillas
>Scut workers
>Nitty-gritty doers
>Detail tenders
>Long-distance runners
>Energetic tryers
>Risk takers
>Sharers
>Team players
>Organizers and mobilizers and
>Servant leaders,

to save our children.

God, please send the right partners for children and the right coworkers for the poor to balance those who speak for powerful adults and rich interest groups.

God, please send new voices for goodness and tolerance to challenge those who teach our children to hate and who prey on our racial and class fears.

God, please bring justice.

So many people feel so overwhelmed and disempowered by the stresses of modern life that they convince themselves they can't make a difference. So they don't even try. They bury their talents in the ground and let their spirits wither on the vine of life. I hope they will bestir themselves at least to say every day as an anonymous old man did: "I don't have the answers, life is not easy, but my heart is in the right place."

It is so important not to let ourselves off the hook or to become apathetic or cynical by telling ourselves that nothing works or makes a difference. Every day, light your small candle. Tutor or mentor or speak to or smile at that one child — your own or one you teach or serve in some way. Every election, take the time to vote for leaders who put children first and against those who don't. Every month decide to write a letter to the editor and to your representatives about a need children have in your community.

The inaction and actions of many human beings over a long time contributed to the crises our children face, and it is the action and struggle of many human beings over time that will solve them — with God's help. So every day, light *your* small candle. It just might be the one that sparks the movement to save our children's and nation's future.

God, please help us remember that all the darkness in the world cannot snuff out the light of one little candle. Help us to keep lighting our little candles until a mighty torch of justice sweeps our nation and the world.

So many times we do not speak up because we do not want to risk criticism or attack. Frederick Douglass correctly upbraided those who wanted change without struggle or discomfort. We must be willing to say and do what is right for our children, whether or not it is politically popular or comfortable for our friends, foes, or peers. Children desperately need adults they can trust to fight for them without thinking of personal consequences when the going gets rough and tough decisions must be made. I was amused when the former and very powerful Ways and Means Chairman Dan Rostenkowski called me and other childcare advocates "bullies" when we brought children and parents to Congress to urge passage of a child care bill. I can't remember them calling powerful corporate executives such names! It is clear that children — who do not vote, lobby, hold press conferences, or make political campaign contributions — will continue to be ignored or marginalized by those in power until a critical mass of caring adults, parents, religious leaders, child advocates, and others build a mighty movement to put children first.

If there is not struggle there is no progress. Those who profess to favor freedom and yet deprecate agitation are men who want crops without plowing up the ground. They want rain without thunder and lightning. They want the ocean without the awful roar of its many waters. This struggle may be a moral one, or it may be a physical one, and it may be both moral and physical, but it must be a struggle. Power concedes nothing without demand. It never did and it never will.

FREDERICK DOUGLASS
"West India Emancipation," 1857

Lord, help me not to fear just or unjust criticism. If they criticized You who were all perfect and good, how can I, neither perfect nor good, expect less?

Lord, take hold of and mold our frail wills, our fainting hopes, our flailing actions, and help us to know there is no evil that You cannot transform to good.

≈⁓ SOMETIMES I forget who is in charge of my life and of our children's cause and get caught up in the ebbs and flows of politics and policy. When child protections that have taken decades of struggle to pass are threatened with repeal or severe budget cuts, I get depressed until I remember to pray. I often gain strength from an episode in Saint Ignatius Loyola's life, related by Alan Paton:

> When his life's work was threatened, St. Ignatius Loyola was asked what he would do if Pope Paul IV dissolved or otherwise acted against the Society of Jesus, to which he had devoted his energy and gifts; and he replied: "I would pray for fifteen minutes, then I would not think of it again."

O God help us to remember that You have the whole world in Your hands—every child in every circumstance everywhere.

OFTEN we procrastinate and make excuses for our inaction, depression, and despair. It's not the right time. I can't make a difference. Whatever I do won't matter. It's not my business. It's somebody else's turn. Nobody will pay attention. It's overwhelming—my little bit doesn't matter.

We must struggle with ourselves and ask God's forgiveness and help to keep being useful in small ways. And we must remember that it is always the right time to do right.

God did not wait till the world was ready,
till . . . nations were at peace.
God came when the Heavens were unsteady,
and prisoners cried out for release.

God did not wait for the perfect time.
God came when the need was deep and great.
God dined with sinners in all their grime,
turned water into wine.

God did not wait till hearts were pure.
In joy God came to a tarnished world of sin and
        doubt.
To a world like ours, of anguished shame
God came,
and God's Light would not go out.

God came to a world which did not mesh
to heal its tangles, shield its scorn.
In the mystery of the Word made Flesh
the Maker of the stars was born.

We cannot wait till the world is sane
to raise our songs with joyful voice,
for to share our grief, to touch our pain,
God came with Love: Rejoice! Rejoice!

MADELEINE L'ENGLE

𑁍 AFTER parents and kin, and along with religious leaders, childcare workers and teachers probably play the most important role in many children's lives. It is ironic that those having the greatest influence on our children's values and development are the least valued by our society. Building big profits and weapons systems rather than big human beings of compassion, achievement, integrity, and discipline continues to take precedence in our national priorities. Even after the fall of Communism, our nation invests far more in military security than in the health, education, job, and personal security of our children, parents, and citizens.

I want people who struggle and work daily for children to know they are valued and are valuable in ways that money or political judgments can never diminish. I hope people who choose to care for children, and whose programs and services are usually cut first and deepest, will carry on anyway. Serving children well is not a job. It is a calling. I do not believe God brought our children's cause this far to let us fail. Carry on for the children you love and touch. They need every encouragement to find their way, however difficult the moment and discouraged you get. *You matter*.

I am so proud that one of my sons is a teacher and that all three sons take time to mentor and tutor children. I hope more parents will encourage their children to see serving others as the highest calling and not make them feel that in order to be important they must become lawyers or doctors or businesspersons or make a lot of money. While any profession can be a route to serving others, I look forward to the time when helping mold precious child minds and spirits is valued as much as or more than making bundles of money. You can't take it with you. And the legacy that ultimately matters will be the values we leave behind in our young.

A CHILDCARE OR CHILD WELFARE WORKER'S LAMENT

Lord, I've got too many children and too few hands
too many demands, too long hours and too little rest
too much noise and too little notice
too much tension and too few thanks
never any peace and not enough pay.

I make less than janitors, parking attendants, and
        garbage collectors
though I help mold the human future every day.

Lord, when is our nation going to come to its senses
        and value those who care for our children?

I get so tired, Lord, trying to maintain order and some semblance of discipline; help me not to forget why I'm here — the children.

Lord, my head aches with the endless tasks of teaching lessons without enough books, science without enough labs, writing without enough pads; I forget why I'm here — the children.

Lord, my spirit sags under the weight of daily struggles nobody appreciates. I yell, I threaten, I throw an eraser, I send off to the principal a rude-mouthed, attention-seeking youth; I forget why I'm here — the children.

My patience is exhausted by year after year of fighting the bureaucracy, parents who don't seem to care, and children who don't seem to learn anything at all. Lord, help me to remember why I'm here — the children.

My energy is drained by too much paperwork, play-ground and cafeteria duty, too many children, too much noise, too many years of beating my head against a wall for too little pay. Lord, help me not to forget why I'm here — the children.

O God, guide my hands in the delivery of this child. Steady my nerves and focus my mind, sharpen my instincts as I help bring this child into the world.

Ease the pain and fear of the mother and the anxiety of the father with anticipation and joy in springing forth a new life.

God, who can turn our worries into wings of joys and our sorrows into songs of thanks, let not our hearts be so troubled by the tragedies of this life's moment that we lose sight of the eternal life in Your Kingdom. Give comfort and solace to our brothers and sisters who suffer almost unbearable losses every second, minute, and hour in our nation and world. Strengthen our resolve to replace hatred with love, tension with trust, and selfishness with caring and community. Heal, O God, all our children so that those who hate and those who are hated, those who hurt and those who are hurt, may grow up in an America and in a world of peace, opportunity, and justice.

WHEN I went to South Africa many years ago to visit women leaders and organizations mobilizing against apartheid, I became deeply depressed after talking to political and civic leaders of all races. Change without a bloodbath appeared impossible. My spirits were revived, though, by three encounters. The first was a secret visit to a banned freedom fighter, Robert Sobukwe, who lay dying in a Cape Town hospital, to take him word of his daughter who was attending Spelman College and living with Andrew and Jean Young in Atlanta. His calm bespoke a man who had completed his portion of God's work on earth and whose soul was at peace. The second encounter was with the young people at the squalid Crossroads shantytown in Cape Town, whose righteous anger, as I knew from my own student days in America's civil rights struggle, would be alleviated only by freedom, regardless of the sacrifice. The third was a visit with a theologian friend at the University of Stellenbosch — the Afrikaner University near Cape Town — when I heard him speak of a flickering effort to begin to redefine apartheid as incompatible with the Dutch Reform theology of the established Afrikaner church.

These three signs made me know that the hidden roots beneath the earth were slowly but surely undergoing transformation and that change would come in God's time with a victim-led grassroots struggle supported by the voices of a prophetic church, personified by Archbishop Desmond Tutu, thousands of sacrificial foot soldiers, and extraordinary leaders like Nelson Mandela and Steve Biko. That the established church was slowly waking up to the oppression of its Black majority was also important.

A PRAYER OF GRATITUDE
FOR MANDELA AND TUTU

Thank You God for Nelson Mandela's unswerving courage, disciplined, steely will, bamboo resiliency, grandfatherly kindness, holy calm, and spirit through imprisonment and freedom. In his presence I am reminded that nothing is impossible if we trust You and faithfully persist.

Thank You God for Desmond Tutu's buoyant spirit and bubbling gurgling laughter that well up from the tip of his toes through the twinkles of his eyes. I feel Your joy in his bouncy joyful presence.

Thank You God for reminding us that racism, poverty, and violence will yield to the faithful moral witness and struggle of men and women and children who would be free — whatever the cost.

Thank You God for the challenge and chance to be moral guerrillas to free our children and nation and world from fear and want and ignorance and prejudice and from the spiritual and physical poverty imprisoning our minds and bodies.

꩜ RACIAL hatred is on the rise at home and abroad. Scapegoating of the weak is increasing. Small welfare babies and immigrants — legal and illegal — are being blamed for all America's woes — real or perceived. People who are different are painted as "un-American." The poor are judged rather than helped as policies allegedly intended to balance the budget and decrease government spending mock the gospel and the prophets who taught that God loved and demanded justice for the poor. I believe the 72nd Psalm's promise that God "shall save the children of the needy, and shall break in pieces their oppressors," and so we must all keep trying all across America and the world — to be His hands and feet and instruments of healing and peace.

God, please help us to remember that what unites us is stronger than what divides us as Americans, as human beings, and as Your children.

And help us, God, to worry less about being politically correct and to seek more to be morally correct by speaking out against injustice wherever it is found.

～ THE world sorts and labels and places different values on children by race, income, religion, color, gender, sexual preference, family status, disability, and other physical, mental, and emotional attributes. We stigmatize children born out of wedlock as "illegitimate" and call children born on the wrong side of the tracks "white trash" or "spics" or "niggers." We act as if IQ (however it is defined) should make a difference in whether a child is protected against hunger, sickness, homelessness, ignorance, violence, neglect, or abuse.

When Christ told His disciples to let the little children "come unto me," He did not say rich children or White children or smart children or nondisabled children. He said let the children come unto me. And so must we.

America's dream is not just for some children—for privileged or White children who did not choose their parents any more than poor Black or Brown or White or homeless children did.

I hope as we raise our own children and debate our public policies as a nation that we will be mindful of the sanctity of each child in God's sight. Whenever we use slurs or stereotypes to demean another or to marginalize any group of children, we weaken our bonds one with the other.

I beg of you to remember that wherever our life touches yours, we help or hinder. Wherever your life touches ours, you make us stronger or weaker. No member of your race in any part of our country can harm the meanest member of mine without the proudest and bluest blood in Massachusetts being degraded. When Mississippi commits a crime, New England commits crime, and in so much, lowers the standard of your civilization. There is no escape — man drags man down, or man lifts man up.

BOOKER T. WASHINGTON
Harvard alumni dinner, 1896

❧

O God of the slave and slave owner
of the exploited and exploiter
of the hated and hater,
teach us to forgive and to love.

It is said that Saint Cyprian of Carthage, the first African bishop martyr, wrote on the Lord's prayer about 250 A.D. that Jesus did not teach us to say "My Father." "The teacher of peace and master of unity did not want prayer to be something individualistic and self-centered. He who inculcated oneness wanted each one to pray for all, just as He Himself bore all as One."

EILEEN AND KATHLEEN EGIN
From *Prayer Times with Mother Teresa: A New Adventure in Prayer*

❦

O God, give us strength to work hard, guidance to work effectively, words to inspire and nourish, and a spirit of cooperation for our children's greater good.

〰 THERE is so much personal and organizational jockeying among people who ought to be working together to serve children, families, and the needy. There is so much to do, there are so many issues left uncovered, so many needs to fulfill. I look forward to the day when each of us finds our thread to weave in a powerful web of advocacy and service for our children.

O God, help us to work together for our children — to use the rich variety of our leaders, organizations, talents, disciplines, and experiences to serve and save our children.

Remind us daily that we and our institutions are the means to serve rather than the ends to be served.

❧ IV ❧

HOLD MY HAND

PRAYERS AND LITANIES
FOR COMMUNITY LEADERS AND
RELIGIOUS CONGREGATIONS

O God, make the door of this house wide enough to receive all who need human love and fellowship, narrow enough to shut out all envy, pride, and strife. Make its threshold smooth enough to be no stumbling block to children, nor to straying feet, but rugged and strong enough to turn back the tempter's power. God, make the door of this house the gateway to Thine eternal Kingdom.

On the door of Saint Stephen's in London

WHILE parents have first and foremost responsibility for taking care of and instilling values in their children, their ability to do so is affected by the policies and values of their nation, culture, and communities, by their economic opportunities in a changing economy, and by the web of support—or lack of it—from religious congregations, schools, employers, and other public and private social support agencies.

I began this book describing the web of values and support among my family, congregation, school, and extended community family of adults who ran Girl and Boy Scout troops, kept children busy in church activities, watched out for children, and considered them a responsibility of the community. Most of my Black community elders did not have a great deal of education and money, but they did have a lot of caring and love and tried to live what they preached. I remember the shocked whispers when someone in the church was thought to be unfaithful to his wife or if a young girl and boy made a mistake and she got pregnant.

What a contrast to many of today's children, who are struggling to grow up without adequate, consistent guidance, protection, and support from enough adults in their lives and who live in a time when divorce and out-of-wedlock births are rampant. As families face increasing stresses of trying to make a living with declining wages or inadequate skills in a postindustrial economy; as more single parents try to raise children alone; as many educators and other service professionals and officials serving children do not live in and feel a stake in the communities in which they work; and as our culture continues to glamorize and normalize gratuitous sex and violence, too many children are growing up fearful and confused. Indeed many adults now fear many of our children and see them as America's problem rather than as America's potential and future.

I believe religious leaders have a special responsibility to provide spiritual guidance and protection for children, and to strengthen parents in their crucial and challenging roles as the first and most enduring and important influence in their children's lives. The most powerful ways that children learn about God's love for them — about trust and unconditional love, about grace and forgiveness, about their invaluable and irreplaceable worth in God's sight — are through the actions of their parents and then through their family of faith and house of worship. How are we fulfilling that promise? Not well enough. Too many congregations are not child- and family-friendly. Religious congregations need to examine their service and witness for our children and families. Too many family and youth ministries are weak or are limited to one day of worship. What is there for the young people to do in your congregation and community during the week? On Friday and Saturday nights? During the summer months? Does your church or temple provide constructive, wholesome alternatives for young people's recreation? What about the young people in your community who are not members of your church, temple, or mosque? Are they welcomed into your house of worship for tutoring, food, recreation, mentoring, and more?

As you consider ways that your congregation can extend its efforts for children, why not start by holding a Children's Sabbath in your congregation? The Children's Defense Fund established the National Observance of Children's Sabbath, in cooperation with a wide range of denominations and religious organizations, to give congregations an opportunity to learn about and faithfully address the needs of children as well as to renew and extend efforts to help them. It is celebrated annually on the third weekend of October in special worship services with prayers, readings, and songs. The Children's Defense Fund provides Children's Sabbath kits for each faith group each year.

I look forward to the day when the religious community in America is the moral locomotive rather than the moral caboose in rising up in righteous indignation to say "enough" and "no more" to the killing, poverty, and neglect of any of God's children. I include in this book prayers and litanies for communities and for religious congregations, which I believe carry a special responsibility for sowing and manifesting through daily action the love, attention, trust, spiritual guidance, and protection that all our children so desperately need.

A PRAYER FOR CHILDREN

O God, we pray for children who woke up this morning in dens of dope rather than in homes of hope, with hunger in their bellies and hunger in their spirits, without parents or friends to care for, affirm, and lovingly discipline them.

Help us to welcome them in our hearts and communities.

We pray for children who have no one to pray for them or protect and guide them and who are being abused or neglected right now by parents who themselves often were abused or neglected.

Help us to welcome them in our hearts and communities.

We pray for children who are sick from diseases we could have prevented, who are dying from guns we could have controlled, and who are killing from rage we could have averted by loving attention and positive alternatives.

*Help us to welcome them in our hearts and
 communities.*

We pray for children struggling to live to adulthood
in the war zones of our cities, who plan their own
funerals and fear each day will be their last. We
mourn for the thousands of children whose life
journeys have already ended too violently and too
soon.

*Help us to welcome them in our hearts and
 communities.*

We pray for children who are born with one, two,
three, or more strikes already against them — too
tiny to live, too sick with AIDS, too addicted to
alcohol or cocaine or heroin to thrive.

*Help us to welcome them in our hearts and
 communities.*

We pray for girl children having children without
husbands or steady friends or lifelines of support,
who don't know how to parent and who need
parenting themselves. And we pray that teen
and adult fathers will take more responsibility
for the children they father.

*Help us to welcome them in our hearts and
 communities.*

We pray for children who are born into and
grow up in poverty without a seat at America's
table of plenty; for youths whose only hope for
employment is drug dealing, whose only sense
of belonging is gangs, whose only haven is the
streets, and whose only tomorrow is prison or
death.

*Help us to welcome them in our hearts and
communities.*

We pray for children and youths in every community
struggling to make sense of life, confused by adults
who tell them one thing and do another; who tell
them not to fight but who fight and tell them not
to take drugs while taking drugs.

*Help us to welcome them in our hearts and
communities.*

O God, we pray for children from whom we expect
too little and for those from whom we expect too
much; for those who have too little to live on and
for those with so much they appreciate little; for
children afflicted by want and for children afflicted
by affluence in a society that defines them by what
they have rather than by who they are — Your
loving precious gift.

Help us to welcome them in our hearts and communities.

We pray for ourselves as parents, teachers, preachers, and leaders, that we will help solve rather than cause the problems our children face, by struggling to be worthy of emulation, since we teach each minute by example.

O God, we pledge to pray and work to save our children's lives.

Help us.

O God, we pledge to pray and work to protect our children's dreams.

Help us.

O God, we pledge to pray and work to rekindle our children's hopes.

Help us.

O God, we pledge to pray and work to rebuild our children's families.

Help us.

O God, we pledge to pray and work to create a sense of community and security for our children.

Help us.

O God, we pledge to pray and work to instill in our
   children a knowledge and appreciation of their
   traditions and heritage.

Help us.

O God, we pledge to pray and work to leave no child
   behind.

Help us.

A COVENANT TO SAFEGUARD
OUR CHILDREN

I. WE COVENANT TO BEAR A MIGHTY MORAL WITNESS FOR CHILDREN

A. We covenant to make a mighty noise and to bear a powerful moral witness to the crisis of violence plaguing our children and to the pressing need to take aggressive action to end it.

B. We covenant to pray, to work, and to reach out each day in peace and love to our children in our homes and communities.

C. We covenant to stand against the tide of guns and violence and poverty and neglect threatening to engulf our children and to stand for and in support of all those things that promote the safe, healthy, and positive development of young people.

D. We each covenant to work to ensure that the killing of a child in our community will not be met with indifference or silence, but rather with a sustained community-wide response to the crisis confronting our children.

E. We covenant to work to find creative ways to capture our community's attention, to disrupt our community's complacency.

II. We Covenant to Be God's Hands, Feet, and Voice for Children

A. We each covenant to take personal responsibility for at least one child in addition to those children who are a part of our regular career and family responsibilities.

B. We each covenant to urge our colleagues, fellow congregants, neighbors, and friends to take personal responsibility for at least one child in addition to those children who are a part of their regular career and family responsibilities.

C. We each covenant to work to ensure that our worshipping community takes a leadership role in efforts to keep its neighborhood safe for children.

D. We each covenant to encourage our worshipping community to establish our neighborhood as a safe haven for children and families.

E. We each covenant to work in partnership with community institutions, organizations, community residents, parents, and other adults to ensure that there is a strong network of safe havens for all children in our community.

F. We each covenant to urge our worshipping community to take its message of hope and renewal into our neighborhood through an active street ministry with young people.

G. We covenant to work together with others to support efforts to address the underlying causes of violence, including poverty, substance abuse, lack of jobs, and the breakdown of the family.

H. We covenant to advocate and encourage others to work for increased investments in effective community initiatives that promote positive youth development.

I. We covenant to work together and encourage others to insist that corporate and government institutions put the interests of children at the top of our local, state, and national agendas.

III. WE COVENANT TO WORK TOGETHER TO GIVE EVERY CHILD A MORAL START

A. We each covenant to work with the faith community to share with our children, by word and example, a strong moral vision that builds community.

B. We each covenant to take an active role in developing community strategies and approaches for teaching children community-building values.

We know that we can carry out this Covenant because of Your promise, as written in the book of Isaiah, that "The mountains shall depart, and the hills be removed; but my kindness shall not depart from thee, neither shall the covenant of my peace be removed, saith the Lord that hath mercy on thee."

Therefore, we covenant to support each other in the

fulfillment of these promises by praying for and with each other, and by generously sharing resources, models, and ideas, and by holding each other accountable. We each covenant to develop and implement each year specific personal and organizational action plans for carrying out this Covenant.

We commit ourselves to this Covenant, cognizant of past faults and in a spirit of reconciliation and healing to fulfill these promises to God, to our children, and to each other.

IN 1994 the Children's Defense Fund bought Alex Haley's 126-acre farm near Knoxville, Tennessee, as a place for spiritual renewal, for character and leadership development, for intergenerational mentoring, and interdisciplinary and interracial communication. I had long dreamed about a place to embody our vision of a renewed extended community family for children — a place where all generations can come and be, reconnect, teach, nurture, be nurtured, and prepare ourselves for saving our children and transforming our families, communities, and nation; a place to mentor and train the new servant-leaders for the 1990s and the twenty-first century; a place to model the behavior we seek to replicate in every community and family; a place to meet and talk and sing and write and dance and laugh and debate and prepare to reenter the world with new energy, a clear shared vision, and new skills for effective action in this era.

I have been struck by how many who have come in the first month of meetings say it feels like home and like the community we have missed. It seems as if the Lord had Alex Haley build, and his estate hold, the farm until our vision ripened and we were ready to embody it in a place. A gurgling creek runs through it, mountains lurk in the background, and trees rustle in the wind while gaggles of geese honk at the lone haughty swan and the ducks who inhabit the pond.

The prayers that follow were a part of the homecoming celebration and dedication in September, 1994.

Lord, we come to this place to remember and celebrate our past, to assess our present, and to prepare for our children's future.

We seek Your help to renew and strengthen the ties that bind and to discard the tares that divide.

We pledge to commit ourselves to work for Your Kingdom on earth by service to the least of these — Your children.

A LITANY OF THANKSGIVING
FOR THE ALEX HALEY FARM

READER: O God, we thank You for this place of beauty and respite, of rivers and pond, of lurking mountains, rolling hills, and level places, of birds and bees, butterflies and bluegill, of ducks and geese and a lone haughty swan.

ALL: Let Your spirit dwell within and among us here and guide all we say and do as we work to leave no child behind.

READER: O God, we thank You for this place of fellowship and faith, of respite and struggle, of silence and community, of listening and sharing, of debating and deciding, of renewal and growth, of planning and action, of good food and good fun.

ALL: Let Your spirit dwell within and among us here and guide all we say and do as we work to leave no child behind.

READER: O God, we thank You for our children—*each* precious in Your sight—whose needs and cause and futures have brought us together here. Help us always to remember that it is not Your will that "even one of these little ones be lost."

ALL: Let Your spirit dwell within and among us here and guide all we say and do as we work to leave no child behind.

READER: O God, we thank You for Alex Haley, who reminded African Americans, and all Americans, of our roots, of our strengths, of our struggles, of our faith, of our God-given human capacity to overcome all adversity and who left us this place of retreat and a life of seeing and affirming the good in others.

ALL: Let Your spirit dwell within and among us here and guide all we say and do as we work to leave no child behind.

READER: O God, we thank You for all those who worked so hard to make today possible, for the donors whose generous sharing enabled us to make this farm a place of hope for our children and for all those who have shared and will

share in large and small ways in the
realization of Your vision for this special place.

ALL: Let Your spirit dwell within and
among us here and guide all we say
and do as we work to leave no child
behind.

READER: And God we thank You for all those
who have worked so hard and so long
for children in our nation. We thank
You for the CDF board and staff and
for the Black Community Crusade
for Children working committee, task
forces, staff, and volunteers. We pray
that You will strengthen their minds
and bodies and spirits to achieve the
work that Your providence assigns
them.

ALL: Let Your spirit dwell within and
among us here and guide all we say
and do as we work to leave no child
behind.

READER: Finally, God, we pray for Your blessings on all who have come to share in
this celebration of thanksgiving and
homecoming. Help us to join together
in a new movement to give every child

a healthy start, a head start, a fair start, a safe start, and a moral start and to leave this place committed to struggle until the prophet Zechariah's vision of "the city full of boys and girls playing in its streets" will be realized again all over our land.

ALL: Let Your spirit dwell within and among us here and guide all we say and do as we work to leave no child behind.

TOGETHER: Let Your work be manifest to Your servants and Your glorious power to their children. Let the favor of the Lord our God be upon us and prosper for us the work of our hands, oh prosper the work of our hands!

A LITANY FOR CHILDREN I

O Lord of light and source of all creation, we praise and glorify You for the children You have given us.

Accept our thanksgiving, O Lord.

For their lives, their inquiring minds and receptive spirits, for their health and growth,

We humbly praise You, O God.

For their beauty and innocence, their laughter and tears, their joyous ways that fill us with wonder and delight,

We humbly praise You, O God.

For their youthful vision by which You lead them trustingly into the future,

We humbly praise You, O God.

For Your constant protection which keeps them safe from harm,

We humbly praise You, O God.

For our families and for Your loving forgiveness
   which allows parents and children to make
   mistakes and, confessing them, to continue to live
   in harmony,

We humbly praise You, O God.

O God of Abraham, Isaac, and Jacob, of Sarah, Rachel,
   and Rebecca, of Your prophets and teachers in
   every time and place, generation after generation
   You call Your children forth to honor and obey
   You.

In awe and gratitude we praise You, O Lord.

For our children's growth in faith and their simple
   trust in You in these complex and troubled times,

We thank You, O Lord.

That Your Spirit will remain with them as they grow,
   guiding them in the ways of justice, righteousness,
   and peace,

We pray to You, O Lord.

For all those who in the faith minister to and teach
   our children and are models of truth and goodness,

We thank You, O Lord.

Defender of the oppressed and the orphan, we pray for all children in our nation and our world who suffer from poverty, injustice, and fear.

Hear the cries of Your children, O Lord.

For children who are runaways, homeless, in institutions, or jails,

In Your tender mercy, protect them, God.

For children who are disabled in mind or body,

In Your tender mercy, encourage and strengthen them, O God.

For children who this day will not have enough to eat,

In Your tender mercy, provide them food, O God.

For babies born at risk, for children who are sick, and for those who lack proper health care, especially pregnant teenagers,

In Your tender mercy, help and sustain them, O God.

For children who are victims of race or class discrimination, poor education, drug or alcohol abuse, and hopelessness,

In Your tender mercy, grant them lives of hope and a future, O God.

For children who daily experience the fear and pain of
war and civil strife, especially the children
of _____,

In Your tender mercy, defend and protect them,
O God.

O God, Loving Parent, we pray for our families and
the families of our nation.

Open our hearts, O Lord.

For children and parents forced to live apart because
of poverty, illness, jail sentences, or migratory
work,

Embrace and uphold them, Spirit of God.

For children and parents enduring the pain and grief
of death or divorce,

Send Your comfort, Spirit of God.

For families facing loss of jobs or the anxiety of an
uncertain future,

Give them hope, Spirit of God.

For children and parents who live in conflict and
misunderstanding,

Give them Your peace and truth, Spirit of God.

For single mothers and single fathers who experience
the burden of raising children alone,

Grant them courage and love, Spirit of God.

O Ruler of all, our sure defense, we pray for the world our children live in and will inherit.

Have pity on us, O Lord.

For the sake of all children, bring an end to the buildup and proliferation of nuclear and other weapons. Preserve us from attitudes and acts that threaten the annihilation of all life and the future we hold in trust for the children.

We cry to You, Creator of all.

For the sake of all children, bring an end to conflict and war between nations. Give us hearts and minds of peace and help us to teach peace to our children.

We cry to You, Creator of all.

For the sake of all children, bring an end to our misuse and pollution of the land, air, and water of the Earth. Teach us to be stewards and guardians of your creation.

We cry to You, Creator of all.

For the sake of all children, bring an end to the injustices caused and abetted by those in places of power. May our hearts and minds be changed by the cries of your hungry and suffering children.

We cry to You, Creator of all.

O Holy God, through whom all things are transformed and made whole, grant us and our children newness of life. Refresh and sustain us with the glorious vision of your world to come in which all children will live in peace and harmony, all children will be filled with good things to eat, and all children will rest secure in your love.

O God Most High, whom we name Yahweh, Lord, and Our Father, Creator, Redeemer, and Sanctifier of the world, we ask these things on behalf of our children and generations yet unborn who will live to praise Your Holy Name, world without end. Amen.

> Written by the Children's Defense Fund for
> National Children's Day, June 1982
> The Washington Cathedral
> Washington, D.C.

O God of infinite love and unending challenge, help us to listen to Your call. Inspire us to use the varied gifts with which we have been blessed in the service of others, especially of children in need.

Keep us ever mindful, we pray, that when we provide adequate nutrition for the children who are hungry, we will have fed Christ.

When we welcome the "strangers" who are children without safe and loving homes, we will have welcomed Christ.

When we donate warm, well-made clothing for the children who are ill-clad, we will have clothed Christ.

When we have immunized all children against preventable disease and ensured adequate health care for all, we will have healed Christ.

When we care for juveniles in custody or the children of people in prison, then, too, we will have visited Christ.

Help us to meet Your challenge and reflect Your love so that one day it might be said that when we did this to the least of them, truly we did it to You.

CHILD 1: Every day in our nation, more than 2,700 babies are born into poverty.

CHILD 2: Every day in our nation, more than 7,400 children are reported abused or neglected.

CHILD 3: Every day in our nation, more than 675 babies are born to mothers who received late prenatal care or none at all.

CHILD 4: Every day in our nation, more than 790 babies are born too small to be healthy.

CHILD 5: Every day in our nation, more than 100 babies die before their first birthday.

LEADER: "A voice is heard in Ramah, lamentation and bitter weeping. Rachel is weeping for her children; she refuses to be comforted for her children, because they are no more."

ALL: *We come together with hearts that weep for our nation's children.*

LEADER: "Thus says the Lord: Keep your voice from weeping, and your eyes from tears; For there is a reward for your work, says the Lord."

ALL: *We come together to be moved from weeping to hear the promise of the work we can do.*

LEADER: "[The children] shall come back from the land of the enemy; there is hope for your future, says the Lord: your children shall come back to their own country."

ALL: *We come together to glimpse your vision of homecoming that would bring our nation's children from an experience of need to one of safety, plenty, and love.*

Be with us in our worship and in our work, O God. Prepare us by the power of Your spirit that we may commit our hearts and hands and minds to realizing Your vision of homecoming for the children of our nation.

Based on Jeremiah 31:15–17

READER: Do you have a vision of God's peace?

ALL: "And the streets of the city shall be full of boys and girls playing in its streets." (Zechariah 8:5)

READER: Do you have a vision of God's peace?

ALL: "[The nations] shall beat their swords into plowshares, and their spears into pruning hooks; nation shall not lift up sword against nation, neither shall they learn war anymore." (Micah 4:3b)

READER: Do you have a vision of God's justice?

ALL: "I will restore the fortunes of my people Israel, and they shall rebuild the ruined cities and inhabit them." (Amos 9:14a)

READER: Do you have a vision of God's justice?

ALL: See, I am going to bring them from the land of the north and gather them from the farthest parts of the earth, among them the blind and the lame, those with child and those in labor, together; a great company they shall return here." (Jeremiah 31:8)

READER: Have you glimpsed God's vision?

ALL: "I will rejoice in Jerusalem, and delight in my people; no more shall the sound of weeping be heard in it, or the cry of distress. No more shall there be in it an infant that lives but a few days, or an old person who does not live out a lifetime." (Isaiah 65:19–20a)

READER: Do you have a vision?

TOGETHER: Yes, we have a vision! Let us gather now to seek God's vision for the children of our world, and God's guidance as we work to pursue it.

For the millions of children who are living in poverty, that despite our society's rejection and inaction, they might feel loved and valuable in your sight.

O God, hear our prayer.

For our nation, that we are moved from tolerance of child poverty to passionate work for justice.

O God, hear our prayer.

For the parents who struggle each day to provide food, pay the rent, keep their families together, and just survive, that they might find community supports that enable them to nurture, enjoy, and spend time with their children.

O God, hear our prayer.

For the children whose needs are unmet, whose cries go unheard, and whose lives hold little joy, that we might fill their needs, respond to their pain, and seek to enrich their lives.

O God, hear our prayer.

For the children who are born too soon or too small, that they will receive the special care that they need, and that our nation will learn from their pain to invest adequately in prenatal care.

O God, hear our prayer.

For the children who are sick and for their parents who don't know how they can pay the bills, that they find care and healing and their parents respite from worry.

O God, hear our prayer.

For our nation's leaders, that they might make children the nation's highest priority, and fulfill the promises that they make to the children.

O God, hear our prayer.

For ourselves, that we might continue, with renewed determination, to serve and advocate on behalf of all children and see that no child is left behind.

O God, hear our prayer.

READER: God is just and merciful. Let us bring our needs and the needs of children and families before God.

For all children, especially the young children who are imperiled by the violence in their homes, neighborhoods, and schools, that they will be comforted and that we will work to make them safe.

ALL: *O God, hear our prayer. Let justice roll down like waters, and righteousness like an everflowing stream.*

READER: For all teenagers, especially the teenagers who are victims and perpetrators of violence, that they are guided safely toward a future of promise and opportunity.

ALL: *O God, hear our prayer. Let justice roll down like waters, and righteousness like an everflowing stream.*

READER: For all parents, especially the parents who struggle in situations of domestic violence and child abuse, that they receive the strength and support they need to protect and nurture their children.

ALL: *O God, hear our prayer. Let justice roll down like waters, and righteousness like an everflowing stream.*

READER: For our elected leaders, that they guide our nation toward a greater manifestation of Your justice, mercy, and peace.

ALL: *O God, hear our prayer. Let justice roll down like waters, and righteousness like an everflowing stream.*

READER: For our nation, that we work to keep our children secure, our families strong, and our neighborhoods safe and leave no child behind.

O God of great faithfulness, we confess that sometimes we feel like giving up, in a world where it seems poverty and violence will always be with us. Our hope succumbs to despair. We confess that sometimes denial and distraction are less painful than vision and commitment. We confess that often we lose our vision—Your vision—of a world where righteousness and peace will kiss each other. We plod through our work and don't dare to dream Your dream of a world made new.

O God whose realm must be entered as a child, we live in a world that looks for results, powerful leaders, and the easy rhetoric of those who proclaim that they have the answer. And we confess that in our rush for results and answers, we forget to listen to the children, the young people, and the parents struggling in poverty and violent communities. We confess that our intentions to work collaboratively are waylaid at times by egos, issues of "territory," racism, sexism, and classism. Sometimes it is hard to acknowledge that we don't know the answer.

O God of hope, renew in us Your vision of a world made new. Mold our hearts and spirits that we might work together and listen for Your word in the voices of the children. Remind us that our only certainty must be eagerness to do Your will. Amen.

Do not be afraid, but let your hands be strong. Speak the truth to one another. Render in your gates judgments that are true and make for peace. Hold only love in your heart for others, and embrace only true commitments.

(Paraphrase of
Zechariah 8:13b, 16–17)

CHILD: All you who are dreamers, too,
Help me make
Our world anew.
I reach out my dreams to you.

READER: Let us go forth to make the world safe for the dreams of children; may we be partners in manifesting God's promised new creation of compassion and justice. Amen.

A PARENT, COMMUNITY, AND NATIONAL AUDIT

IT IS TIME for adults of every race and income group to break our silence about the pervasive breakdown of moral, family, and community values, to place our children first in our lives, and to struggle to model the behavior we want our children to learn. Our "youth problem" is not a youth problem, it is an adult problem, as our children do what they see us adults doing in our personal, professional, and public lives. They seek our attention in negative ways when we provide them too few positive ways to communicate how to get the attention and love they need.

I urge every parent and adult to conduct a personal audit to determine whether we are contributing to the crisis our children face or to the solutions they urgently need. Our children don't need or expect us to be perfect. They do need and expect us to be honest, to admit and correct our mistakes, and to share our struggles about the meanings and responsibilities of faith, parenthood, citizenship, and life. Before we can pull up the moral weeds of violence, materialism, and greed in our society that are strangling our children, we must pull up the moral weeds in our own backyards.

So many children are confused about what is right and wrong because so many adults talk right and do wrong in our personal, professional, and public lives.

- If we are not supporting a child we brought into the world as a father or as a mother with attention, time, love, discipline, money, and the teaching of values, then we are a part of the problem rather than the solution to the family breakdown today that is leaving so many children at risk.
- If we are abusing tobacco, alcohol, cocaine, or other drugs while telling our children not to, then we are a part of the problem rather than the solution in our overly addicted society.
- If we have guns in our home and rely on them to feel safe and powerful, and don't stand up to those who market guns to our children and to those who kill our children, or glamorize violence as fun, entertaining, or normal, then we are a part of the problem rather than the solution to the escalating war of American against American, family member against family member, that is tearing us apart.
- If we tell our daughters not to engage in premature and irresponsible sex, and not to have children before they are prepared to parent and support them, and do not tell our sons the same thing, then we are a part of the problem rather than the solution to teen pregnancy and out-of-wedlock births so many decry.

- If we send rather than take our children to Sunday school and worship services, and believe that the Sermon on the Mount, the Ten Commandments, the Koran, or whatever religious beliefs we hold, pertain only to one-day worship but not to Monday through Sunday home, professional, and political life, then we are a part of the problem rather than the solution to the spiritual famine plaguing America today.

- If we tell, snicker, or wink at racial, gender, religious, or ethnic jokes or engage in or acquiesce in any practices intended to diminish rather than enhance other human beings, then we are contributing to the proliferating voices of racial and ethnic division and intolerance staining our land again. Let's not go through the civil war and civil rights movement all over again. Let's not repeat the worst lessons of our past. Let's prepare for the future.

- If we think being American is about how much we can get rather than about how much we can give and share to help our children get a healthy, fair, and safe start in life, then we are a part of the problem rather than the solution.

- If we think it's somebody else's responsibility to teach *our* children values, respect, good manners, and work and health habits, then we are a part of the problem rather than the solution to parental neglect today.

- If we or our organizations are spending more money

on alcohol and entertainment than on scholarships, books, tutoring, rites of passage, and mentoring programs for youths, then we are a part of the problem rather than the solution to ensuring positive alternatives for children.

- If we'd rather talk the talk than walk the walk to the voting booths, school board meetings, political forums, and congregation and community meetings to organize community and political support for our children, then we are a part of the problem rather than the solution.

- If our children of any color think that being smart and studying hard is acting White rather than acting Black or Brown and don't know about the many great Black and Brown as well as White achievers who overcame every obstacle to succeed, then we are a part of the problem rather than a part of the solution to racial stereotyping.

- If we are not voting and holding political leaders accountable for investing relative pennies in Head Start and pounds in the defense budget, and for opposing welfare for poor mothers and children while protecting welfare for rich farmers and corporate executives, then we are a part of the problem rather than the solution to the growing gap between rich and poor.

- If we think corrupt and unaccountable Black and Brown leaders who neglect our children and communities are better than corrupt and unaccountable

White leaders who neglect our children and communities or vice versa, then we are a part of the problem rather than the solution to voter cynicism and apathy.

- If we think we have ours and don't owe any time or money or effort to help those left behind, then we are a part of the problem rather than the solution to the fraying social fabric that threatens all Americans.

GUIDE MY FEET

꧁ A FEW summers ago, my husband and I and two friends set out one morning in the Swiss Alps on what we thought was going to be a beautiful but easy walking excursion. The plan was to take the cable car to the top of the Fee (Fairy Mountain) at Saas Fee — about ten thousand feet high — enjoy the beautiful view, tour the inside of the glacier carved out by hearty souls of old, eat a snack, walk across the glacier, and then walk down to the cable car I thought was at the next landing. I expected to return to our hotel by early afternoon for a leisurely read before dinner. We all had worn our ankle-high walking shoes.

The first part went as planned. The Psalmist David's sense of awe "Oh come and see what God has made" flowed through me in the humbling presence of such majestic mountain peaks. As the sun shone down on the snowcapped mountains where skiers frolicked and mountain climbers fearlessly trudged upwards, I marvelled at the contrast of so much sun and so much snow in July.

As we began our trek home across the glacier, our progress turned out to be slower and harder than anticipated as melting water running down the mountain made traction a bit tricky. After walking carefully for about an hour, we were happy to stop at a small hut for hot coffee before descending through the beautiful field of snow below to catch the cable car.

The field of snow turned out to be both deeper and longer than it appeared from afar. We had to step carefully in the knee-deep white mass lest an ankle or foot twist on the uneven ground. Moving like a marching toy soldier, lifting high my legs, I found myself tiring and getting a bit panicked as my feet got colder and colder from their snowy immersion and as the distance to travel seemed farther and farther. After nearly an hour's descent, we finally came — a bit shaken and cold — into a beautiful green clearing where mountain goats grazed near streams flowing between huge boulders and rocks. As I looked back from where we had come, I felt a sense of both relief and accomplishment.

I looked for and did not see the cable car but walked on across the rocks and up a gentle winding mountain path. After fifteen minutes or so it dawned on me that the path was going up and up. I have a great fear of ledges — which an Outward Bound experience helped me temporarily conquer — so I began to talk to myself as the mountain stretched high ahead. I looked back, wondering if I could retrace my steps up the field of snow and back across the glacier to our original departure point, but knew I had to forge ahead. I envisaged the cable car around the next mountain bend and told myself to look at the extraordinary beauty of God's gifts all around and not to look down. A hearty hiker who had come from the direction in which we were headed saw my fear and told me just to put one foot ahead of the other and to keep moving. So I kept going, very slowly at times. But the mountain went on and on and got higher and higher and the ledges seemed more menacing and the rocks more formidable. Hour after hour it continued. I felt sorry that our friends had been subjected to such a grueling test on their first day's vacation with us and hoped they would forgive us. We kept our eyes on each other as one or the other lagged but kept moving — searching for the cable car home.

As the day began to wane, I started to fear that we might be caught on the mountain at dark or miss the cable car. Finally, a hiker appeared with the news that the last car was at five o'clock and we could make it if we walked very fast. Adrenalin wiped away my fatigue as I contemplated trekking down thousands more feet. We reached the cable landing a few minutes before that last car left.

This mountain adventure trip is a metaphor of sorts for me in my lifelong struggle for children. The quest to put children first has required climbing mountain after mountain with no end in sight. But we must not despair. Child advocates must keep moving, putting one foot ahead of the other, basking in the beauty of our children, in the chance to serve and engage in a struggle for a purpose higher than ourselves, and continue to work and pray hard. I have no doubt we will catch our cable car to success one day. It will require climbing many more difficult mountains and endless hard work. It will require a joining together of people from all walks of life who seek something bigger and better than material things, soulless technology, and power. And it will require personal and collective transformation and commitment by you and me to build a safe and loving world for every child—however long it takes. Gandhi was right when he said:

> If we are to teach real peace in this world and if we are to carry on a real war against war, we shall have to begin with children; and if they will grow up in their natural innocence, we won't have to struggle; we won't have to pass fruitless, idle resolutions, but we shall go from love to love and peace to peace, until at last all the corners of the world are covered with that peace and love for which, consciously or unconsciously, the whole world is hungering.
>
> MAHATMA MOHANDAS GANDHI
> India, November 19, 1931

MARIAN WRIGHT EDELMAN is founder and president of the Children's Defense Fund, widely considered our most effective national voice for children, and the author of the *New York Times* bestseller, *The Measure of Our Success: A Letter to My Children and Yours.* A graduate of Spelman College and of the Yale Law School, Edelman has won numerous awards for her work, including a MacArthur Prize Fellowship and the Albert Schweitzer Humanitarian Award. She and her husband, Peter Edelman, have three grown sons and live in Washington, D.C.

7